THE
VIRTUES
OF AN
AUTHENTIC
LIFE

For Flass —
Continue on your own
Authentic Journey —
God will open the Doors —
Your hope, Spirit and
Ment will take you
To your Destination —

Love DAD
ATZOMITA
31 July
2002

THE
VIRTUES
OF AN
AUTHENTIC
LIFE

*A Celebration of
Spiritual Maturity*

BERNARD HÄRING

Translated by Peter Heinegg

Liguori
LIGUORI, MISSOURI

Published by Liguori Publications
Liguori, Missouri

Library of Congress Cataloging-in-Publication Data

Häring, Bernard, 1912–.
  [Grundplan erfüllten Leben. English]
  The virtues of an authentic life : a celebration of spiritual ma-
turity / Bernard Häring : translated by Peter Heinegg.
      p. cm.
  ISBN 0-7648-0120-1
  1. Christian life. 2. Virtues. I. Title.
BV4501.2.H339713   1997
241'.4—dc21   97-12992

Copyright © 1997 by Bernard Häring
Printed in the United States of America
First U.S. Edition
01 00 99 98 97   5 4 3 2 1

Contents

Foreword   ix

Part One   1
   1. Virtue As Competence   3
   2. A Critical Decision:
     Choosing a Life of Virtue   7
   3. Freely Chosen Virtue   11
   4. Virtue and the Competent Conscience   16
   5. The Greatest of Virtues   20

Part Two   25
   6. Faith: Belief in Love Victorious   27
   7. Hope: Love-Filled Confidence   30
   8. Justice: A Creation of Love   34
   9. Prudence: The Vigilant Eye of Love   38
  10. Courage: A Gift of Love   42
  11. Moderation: Measuring by Love's Standard   45
  12. Compassion: The Image of God's Love   49
  13. Creative Fidelity: A Mark of True Love   53

Part Three   59

14. The Virtue of Gratitude   61
15. Alertness: A Response to the
    Grace of Gratitude   65
16. The Virtue of Discernment   69
17. Perseverance   74
18. Living on an Advance of Trust   77
19. The Virtue of Contrition   82
20. The Virtues of Patience and Holy Impatience   85
21. Cultivating the Virtue of Healthy Doubt   89
22. The Cheerful Virtue of Joy   92
23. The Precious Virtue of Humor   95
24. Irony and Satire As Christian Virtues   99
25. The Virtue of Enthusiasm   102
26. Generosity   106
27. Frugality   110

Part Four   115

28. The Virtue of Just Kindness, or *Epikeia*   117
29. The Virtue of Reciprocity   121
30. Tolerance   125
31. Nonviolence   129
32. Humility: More Than a Moth-Eaten Virtue   133
33. The Virtue of *Kenosis*: Gain Through Loss   137
34. Magnanimity   141
35. Noble-Mindedness   145
36. Serenity   148
37. The Virtue of Frankness, or *Parrhesia*   153
38. The Virtue of Grown-Up Obedience   157

39. Truthfulness   161
40. Sincerity: A Sign of Upright Behavior   165
41. Openness   169
42. The Virtue of Chastity   172
43. The Virtue of Childlikeness   175
44. The Virtue of Aging With Dignity   178

Foreword

This book would never have been written without Father Joseph Cascales, the editor of the Cursillo magazine *Erlebtes Evangelium* (*Living the Gospel*). Over the course of the last few years, he kept asking me for brief essays on one virtue or another. Finally, I decided to complete the series and shape it into a whole. I found the work stimulating, and so I hope that reading it—that is, meditating on this basic plan for a full life—will prove stimulating, too.

PART ONE

1

Virtue as Competence

Is virtue one of those humorless, haggard, tooth-less aspects of life that just have to be endured and reckoned with, whether we like it or not? Absolutely not. Virtue is, instead, a form of competence that enables us to grasp the melody of life as a whole and to arrive at that basic option for good that brings all of our thoughts, desires, and actions to maturity.

Almost everybody admits that competence in one's profession is worth the effort it takes. And, competence in relationships is a central goal of many others as well. When competence in any sphere is lacking, when the struggle to get it is neglected, the price will be high. The frequent breakdown of marriage, with all its costly consequences, is one tragic example. Many people realize that, before the wedding, a couple has to become as competent as possible in preparation for this great adventure. The learning process only begins at marriage; the struggle for additional competence continues as spouses become parents and grow together through the other stages of marriage.

Virtue is a much more comprehensive and profound sort

of competence than professional or relationship competence. In fact, it guarantees that our personal life, our life with others, and even our death, will be completely meaningful.

The issue at stake here is nothing less than moral competence. We are talking about the value and nobility of the human person as an individual and in his or her life and work together with others. Our goal is nothing less than true, inner freedom to achieve the Good, the True, and the Beautiful. In pursuing a life of virtue, we are seeking an impeccable quality of individual conscience, as well as a way for the individual conscience to work successfully with and for one another. We are trying to become a person in possession of a mature conscience and, even more, a person with a most inwardly dynamic and accurate conscience.

Without virtue, everything is hollow and dull. Indeed, without virtue, men and women are good for nothing and public dangers. The healthy veneration of ancestors in Africa is built around the common, grateful memory of the virtues of forbears, virtues that people keep telling and retelling, celebrating and recelebrating, in the rhythmic flow of the year. This veneration imparts a taste for virtue in both the present and in the upcoming generation. The individual man or woman, the family, the clan, the tribe, the whole people—all live on the treasure of virtue accumulated by and through the ancestors, whose virtues enrich and ennoble the life of the community.

The veneration of the saints serves the same lofty goal in Western culture, as do good biographies of holy and exemplary persons. Virtue is not just an abstraction. It lives and wants to be lived.

Virtue is always concerned with the whole, with the personality as a whole, and with the whole personality in the context of all of its healthy and healing human relationships.

We are likewise becoming more aware that wherever true virtue is at home we also have strong, healthy, happy relations with nature and with the whole of creation. What kind of "paragons of virtue" are those who plunder and poison our vulnerable planet with their brutal and ruthless exploitation? This brutality that requires a counter concern for the welfare of our earth shows us that nowadays the word *virtue* implies a great many demands. At stake is nothing less than everything, not just virtue, but *all* virtues, that together sing the hymn of the redeemed—hymns that sustain and radiate peace, joy, freedom, and solidarity.

As you consider the following chapters, dear reader, be critical and test whether and to what extent this little effort speaks competently about the most important kind of human competence. You will also, of course, read *self*-critically. There will be stretches where you will enjoy yourself and say: Here I'm really on the way to complete competence. But if you read carefully, you will sometimes find yourself saying: Here I really have to—and I will—wake up and see how I can become *more* competent. As you read on, it will become perfectly clear to you that virtue amounts to the highest and most important competence in your life and in the lives of all those who are personally dear to you or entrusted to your care.

Perhaps, by the time you finish the book, you may feel in your heart a yearning to acquire the highest and most indispensable competence and to help others gain it. If so, then perhaps you will begin rereading, so as to get a complete and detailed picture of the highest human competence, of *your* competence, and to struggle to achieve it day after day. This effort will benefit your relations with God, your neighbor, your profession, as well as benefiting your private and social life.

It has to be said, though, as plainly as possible, that behind this effort to achieve competence through virtue lies a further goal—the change in paradigm from a one-sided ethic of obedience to a dedicated ethic of responsibility. This further approach declares war on conformism and on a lust for control of both people and things. Once we have unequivocally rejected any sort of ethic of blind obedience, we will see that obedience still counts as a noble virtue for the Christian adult. But it now takes on a new form: the form of listening to one another, listening as a community to God, and heeding the signs of the times.

2

A Critical Decision: Choosing a Life of Virtue

We cannot really and truly decide in favor of any particular virtue until we have reached a thorough, radical decision to commit ourselves to opt for goodness in the whole of our lives and in all our relations.

Moral theologians and moral psychologists have recently been paying closer attention to this point—this option for goodness as a whole. At issue here is a fundamental choice in regard to the overall purpose and total meaning of our lives and the lives of our fellow men and women. It is no accident that Saint Thomas Aquinas, in his ethical writings, pays so much attention to the question of this final goal, this *finis ultimus*.

Without this overriding vision, the individual virtues quickly degenerate into a toothless and repellent caricature. Each individual virtue has to find a home in the total domain of all virtues. And it is this constellation of virtues working together that is precisely what is meant by the "basic option," or "critical decision." This decision is not an isolated or supplementary one, but a decision in favor of the most intimate and dynamic principle of moral goodness and resolution. The basic option is simply the principle behind all our moral efforts. This central principle endows our moral efforts with unity, wholeness, authenticity, and the power to grow.

Occasionally, for all their good will and good intentions, people fail in some difficult area, for example, patience with oneself or others. But if they do not give up the fight, then the unity provided through their overall decision, their dedication to the basic option, can help them continue striving for the virtue in question. Their determination is shored up by their previous chosen option for the Good.

Often enough, people who are essentially good and eager to do the right thing remain half blind or asleep at the wheel when it comes to some personal flaw. This isolated failure does not necessarily call into question the genuineness or authenticity of their moral character or of their decision to follow the basic option for goodness. However, if on the occasion of an unpleasant and perhaps even humiliating failure, a person has a full awakening, then he or she faces a full reappraisal of everything. Either the ongoing basic option for the good will prompt a fresh burst of strength to bring order in this direction. Or else, if that person turns away from such a challenge, then there will also be a total reappraisal, but a negative one. In this case, the basic option is uprooted and can even end up reversing itself.

The struggle to reach the basic decision, to have it take root and achieve full fertility, is what makes the personality authentic, reliable, and increasingly radiant.

Overzealousness or even fanaticism in the area of a particular virtue—for example, exalting chastity, while simultaneously being blind or insensitive to other, possibly more important, things—makes such "virtue" suspicious. Worse, yet, fanaticism makes virtue look nasty, like a sort of contagious disease, the enemy of happiness, or harmony, and of success in general.

In an ethic with a lopsided stress on blind obedience, all the talk about virtue makes the very subject a source of irritation and contempt. Preachers and practitioners of such "virtue" can all too easily give virtue a bad name, unless it is made completely clear to them—and to ourselves—that their sermons and preaching are off the mark: virtue has nothing to do with going to obedience school.

Correct understanding and faithful efforts to make a basic decision for the practice of virtue and to root it more solidly in the whole of the personality are the best advertisements for the common aspiration to competence in the area of the Good, the True, and the Beautiful. Virtue becomes the most fascinating expression of beauty precisely through its perceptible dynamism, aimed at wholeness and authenticity.

Authenticity is a key word whenever morality, ethics, and virtue are concerned. An artist could write a striking book on the aesthetics of virtue, or moral goodness. A good number of "the silent," both as individuals and as a group, could serve as a tremendous exemplars of goodness and authenticity, which are precious embodiments of the Beautiful. That is the point of the traditional thesis that the True, the Good, and the Beautiful are inseparable and "transcendental." Together, they constitute the splendor and happiness of a successful life—one that overcomes banality and isolation.

3

Freely Chosen Virtue

The abstract concept of freedom says nothing about the domain of virtue. But the good arising out of the possibility of inward freedom serves the cause of the individual and the community. Virtue sings freedom's praises. The kind of freedom being discussed here has nothing to do with the capricious whims of human variability nor with freedom as a breaking away from order and responsibility.

The moral freedom enjoyed by human beings is the greatest risk God ever took, a risk without which his creation would have been something altogether different. It would lose both its greatness and its tragedy.

God himself is all freedom because he is all truth, all goodness, and all love. God is altogether himself in his freedom to communicate his truth and his goodness. He has done this through creation by which he has endowed human beings with minds and with free will. But this freedom, because it is created, can also bring failure: free, guilty failure, the failure of saying *no* to God—the Good, the True, and the Beautiful.

How could God run such a risk? Creaturely freedom, just because it is creaturely and hence fragile, includes the possibility of failure, a refusal to accept the Good, the True, and the Beautiful. This refusal, in the final analysis, means the possibility of refusing God himself. Here we catch a glimpse of the "mystery of sin," the incomprehensible, shattering mystery of the *no* that the creature can say to the Good, and the True, and, hence ultimately, to God himself.

God freely dares to endow creatures with the fragile gift of freedom, even with the freedom of total disobedience by which his creatures can say *no* to the source of all freedom. Is not this total freedom something similar to the fullness of God's virtue?

Given this similarity, we can only adore, be amazed, and fall silent in awe. Anything we could say would simply be stammering.

God somehow suffers, too, as he views the suffering of his creatures. Above all, he suffers as he watches the stupid, truculent way in which they gamble with their freedom. This gambling creates a risk of the highest magnitude, because with every *no* said to the Good, the True, and the Beautiful, the freedom to affirm this very Good, True, and Beautiful is lessened. This gambling with *no* is a loss in and of itself, a loss that can turn into a total loss unless God once again intervenes with a "new creation." The people who gamble with and gamble away their freedom are wounding all of creation, but above all they are wounding themselves.

In this instance, the other unfathomable mystery of God makes its appearance. God answers this creaturely *no* from the bottomless depths of his goodness and truth with a compassion that ultimately must be understood as a healing mercy. "Be merciful, just as your Father is merciful" (Lk 6:36). God's mercy include a pain-filled sympathy with the sinner.

Though God is exalted above all creation, this exaltedness is something quite different from what we find in the ancient philosophers Plato and Aristotle. Their perfect, all-powerful "God" remains completely untouched by our *no*, by our self-enslavement. Our Christian God *is* touched, and this hurt comes not from us but from God's innermost mystery of love. He has the total freedom to love, even freedom vis-à-vis the sinner.

God's compassion—his suffering with us—reaches its high point in the Incarnation of the Word of God and, finally, in Jesus' sorrowful dying on the cross. The nature of this divine freedom is given matchless expression, in the highest sense, by Jesus' prayer on the cross: "Father, forgive them; for they do not know what they are doing" (Lk 23:34), and in his last word of the greatest freedom, "Father, into your hands I commend my spirit" (Lk 23:46).

In view of God's unheard-of daring in giving freedom to rational creatures, who could then refuse him and his love? Faced with this mystery, we can only stand amazed and grope with uncertainty toward a deeper understanding. In the light of this mystery, before which we can only mutter helplessly, it nevertheless becomes brilliantly clear that God's freedom is virtue to the highest degree. It is a free emanation of love in the compassionate bringing home of men and women to the true kingdom of freedom.

The fact that our freedom and our incomprehensible redemption originate from God's compassion plainly shows us that our grateful *yes* to this mystery becomes our freedom to do good—a doing that includes repentance and conversion. This capacity, indeed, is an inconceivable, magnificent sort of competence and is part of the very foundation and treasury of our freedom.

We have the freedom to say a free, faithful *yes* to God's daring risk in endowing us with the ability to repent, to convert, and to choose a new life. Our choice of this new life as citizens of the Kingdom of God is virtue in its highest capacity. This freedom of the children of God is not just any run-of-the-mill virtue, but the highest of all virtues—a true moral competence.

This virtue puts an irrevocable stop to slavish obedience, as well as to every way of manipulating freedom that invokes an ethic of slavish obedience. Utter villains, such as Hitler and Stalin, along with their henchmen, would probably not have had such an easy time of it if Christian churches and Christian educators had placed more stress on the exercise of competent freedom and on a comprehensive and deeply based ethic of responsibility. Placed within this framework and seen in the light of virtue as a competence, authentic obedience flourishes. At the core of authentic obedience is hearing and heeding one another as together we listen to and heed God and the signs of his presence.

Bearers of authority who wangle obedience out of people with every available control device and with a clever mixture of rewards and punishments do not deserve an audience. And, in the long run, they will not be listened to, certainly not by those who use their God-given freedom competently and who constantly bring it to bear on their lives as much as possible.

For the convinced Christian who has been called to adulthood, there is no going back to a one-sided ethic of obedience. Grown-up Christians will not try to pass off their responsibility to their superiors and to those in power.

Only in terms of a joint and thankful effort to cultivate competence in the use of freedom can we carry out the paradigm change from a one-sided ethic of obedience to a practiced ethic of responsibility. That is the gift and task of freedom.

Anyone who wants to continue staking everything on the obedience ethic—whether as a person in authority or as a subordinate—can spare himself or herself the trouble of reading this book. Rather, this volume is quite consciously aimed at those concerned about their own personal and, at the same time, group competence in the use of freedom.

We have to give an account before God and in the light of our own consciences, not just of the claims of obedience but of our willingness—or daring—to obey. For this and for much else, we need a competent conscience, one that includes not just the necessary knowledge, but, above all, virtue in its most comprehensive sense. Only then will we find fulfillment in our freedom as children of God.

4

Virtue and the Competent Conscience

With our conscience we stand before God, who is the ultimate source of everything good and, not in the least, the source of our freedom. Invoking one's own conscience in order to justify a decision is easy, but achieving a thoroughly competent conscience is an enormous task that is never fully finished.

When the conscience is awake and alert, we know about ourselves, about our freedom, and about our calling to the redeemed and redeeming love that comes from God and leads back to him. Our conscience is healthy when we can clearly discern what is true freedom and what is owed to the global kingdom founded on love. We must look closely and see whether and how far our thoughts, desires, and actions serve our common—but still altogether personal—calling to the freedom we possess as the children of God.

The formation of an alert conscience has a lot to do with *existential knowledge*—a knowledge of true freedom. Existential knowledge is a comprehensive competence for recognizing, loving, and doing everything useful for the kingdom of God. It embraces true love, justice, and, not the least of all, our mission of peace.

But knowledge alone is by no means the whole story. The way that we know about ourselves and the Good is largely dependent on our *character*. By that I mean not our temperaments (choleric, sanguine, or so on), but our general level of competence anchored in the totality of the virtues. Our character depends on what place we assign to the individual virtues in our lives. What do we truly value? What is our attitude toward virtue? How steady is our response to the demands of virtue. We possess a competent character if it is built on a solid and unequivocally understood basic decision for good. In the consolidated character of the individual, all the virtues in the basic option unite and work together.

Character formation is our greatest task in life. We form our character with a view to our vocation and mission. It is never just one person's private undertaking, but a striving together with and for one another. Character formation is not a supplementary task, alongside the effort to achieve a competent conscience but our core concern. It is the means by which we flourish in our freedom as God's children.

The kind of knowledge we seek and its context helps to determine the competence of a person's conscience. What sort of knowledge is the dominant kind in me? Is it a *salvific knowledge,* that is, an existential knowledge about what makes for salvation, what makes me and my relations healthy and healing?

Is *generic* or *common knowledge* paramount in my personality, that is, knowledge that comes from a general education. Is this generic knowledge balanced as far as values and usefulness go? Is it coordinated with a global view of reality? Or is it a colorful chaos where the important things are swamped by trivialities?

Both our salvific knowledge and the competence of our conscience are particularly threatened by a proliferation of *dominating knowledge,* that is, the kind of knowledge and skill through which I gain my own advantage over other people, the community, my subordinates, or those entrusted to me for education or pastoral care. One example of the many varieties of dangerous dominating knowledge is the art of working one's way to the top, whatever the cost to others. One sees this kind of knowledge when clerics slyly pursue their "careers" in an all-too-hierarchical religious institution, or in the way those devoted to success clamber to the top reaches of corporate power.

The most dangerous dominating knowledge, one that bypasses the autonomy of the competent conscience, is the shameless art of cleverly mixing promises with threats and mixing rewards with punishments in order to manipulate the consciences of other people. This method seeks to trap the unwary in a kind of obedience that is neither responsible nor adult, but an obedience that is useful to the manipulator.

The competence of our conscience is also largely determined by the care we give to our *memory*. A person's memory is a sanctuary when it is filled with healthy gratitude for one's own blessings, with thankful recollections of good experiences, and with praise for God's wondrous deeds in salvation history. But memory can also turn into a dumping ground with a frightful tangle of poisonous and less poisonous memories along with only a few usable memories. The competence of our conscience is shattered when memory becomes a den of thieves, where rage, strife, bitterness, and implacable resentment gradually drive out every sort of salvific knowledge, praise, and gratitude.

To sum up briefly: our efforts to achieve a competent conscience necessarily include the formation of character, the cultivation of salvific knowledge and an orderly general knowledge, and, lastly, the careful fostering of a healthy memory.

5

The Greatest of Virtues

The virtue that is spoken of in the title of this chapter is not to be understood in the first instance as one that we have acquired or are to acquire in the future. Rather, it is to be understood as the greatest, most precious, and most powerful force that we know. That which leads us to disciplined freedom and a competent conscience is the undeserved love that God has given us.

This kind of love will not let itself be pocketed. It comes and willingly abides with us only if we receive it as a guest. The greatest love is not that with which we begin to love, but the love that knocks on our door, that wants to enter and stay with us. This love is part of the core message of the New Testament: "God loved us first"; and "He loved us when we were still sinners."

This love, a love that wants to come and stay with us, deserves and demands our grateful attention. In chapter 13 of 1 Corinthians, Paul admonishes us to open ourselves to this gift and to tend it carefully. We cannot just cultivate it on the side, so to speak. This love wants to be recognized and prized as the queen of virtues. "If I speak in the tongues of mortals and of angels, but do not have love, I am a noisy gong or a clanging cymbal" (13:1). Indeed, even if we knew everything and could do everything, the rule would still hold: "If...I do not have love, I am nothing" (13:2). In this context, Paul's immediate concern is to show the true face, the actual identity, of this love (13:4–8).

In the following chapters I will follow closely in the footsteps of Paul, the apostle to the Gentiles. I will try to point out the irreplaceable features of redeemed and redeeming love and, in other words, the competent human freedom that has been redeemed.

Here is a summary of that redeeming love and its consequences.

Love is the heart and eye of faith.

Love radiates trust and hope.

Love gives rise to prudence, which is the watchful eye of love.

Redeemed love guarantees strength of spirit and true courage; boundless love teaches moderation.

The love that comes from God is compassionate, full of sympathy.

Those who give themselves to this love radiate joy and peace.

Love itself gives perseverance in the service of this love.

Love brings about a kind of *kenosis* or emptying: a letting go of everything that stands in the way of love.

Love turns loss into gain.

Love is creatively faithful.

Love overflows in gratitude and makes us ready to serve.

Love watches alertly for the opportunity of each moment.

Love pours out the gift of discernment.

Love alone can bring us perseverance in the service of God.

Love stands amazed at the advance of God's love and returns it.

Love nurtures repentance in a constantly deepening conversion.

Love creates a fruitful synthesis of holy patience and impatience.

Love frees us from senseless doubt and makes even doubt fruitful.

Love radiates gaiety and is infectious in the best sense.

Love awakens and nourishes humor, the gentle smile of love.

Love lives on enthusiasm and spreads it.

Love is generous because it experiences itself as a gift.

Love expresses itself in contagious frugality.

Love synthesizes healing gentleness (*epikeia*) and zeal for the law.

Love engenders the capacity for genuine reciprocity and counters evil and fanaticism with tolerance.

Through nonviolence, love makes us into true disciples of Jesus.

Love has its preferred meeting point in humility.

Love is an emptying of self (*kenosis*) in union with Jesus.

Love is cheerful in every way and nurtures magnanimity and every sort of greatheartedness.

Love proves its power in serenity.

Through its frankness, love unmasks cowardice and lies.

Love breeds adult obedience and is in every way truthful and transparent.

Love teaches uprightness, the virtue of sincerity.

Love is openness to everything that comes from love and leads to it.

Love is truly chaste and unmasks every sort of shamelessness.

Love makes us rich in every way yet also is frugal.

Love teaches us to grow old with dignity and to let go. This letting go is part of the crucial art, the art of dying (*ars moriendi*) happily.

Lastly, love conquers in life and in death.

PART TWO

6

Faith: Belief in Love Victorious

Our Christian faith, this incomprehensibly precious gift of God, must not be thought of as a virtue that we achieve on our own. Faith is a pure, unearned gift. The Holy Spirit, the ground and giver of all good gifts, creates faith in us and brings it to fulfillment, provided that we honor this gift *as* a gift.

For our part, faith is a thankful, adoring reception accompanied by a pure heart—a reception that becomes a response of praise. The gift of faith bears fruit according to the measure of our dedication to God, to his Gospel, and to his kingdom of grace and love. And, not the least of all, this grateful and adoring reception will be expressed by our taking all pains to meditate lovingly on the Good News.

Faith comes from hearing. The truly believing Christian is all eyes and ears. The knowledge of faith is not just another form of knowledge. It is the knowledge of salvation: boundless veneration for the infinitely greater mystery of God.

Faith is traditionally called a theological virtue. To the degree that we open ourselves in gratitude to this virtue of faith, it irradiates and warms all our thoughts and wishes.

Christian faith looks, above all, to Jesus. He is the pure mirror in which we look with amazement at God's fatherly love. The infinitely exalted God reveals himself in faith in his affection and care for us—an affection that is both motherly and fatherly.

In the light of faith, constantly nurtured with the Gospel, everything takes on a new look, a new depth and height. Creation then becomes infinitely more than a thing, more than a commodity. Through faith we can see God's glory, sublimity, wisdom, and beauty shining through in all creation.

Faith shows us our nobility, our sublime dignity. But a faith-filled people will not begin to get a sense of their own calling and dignity through the possession of this virtue until they also see and honor their fellow men and women, particularly those that are the least of them and the most despised. Faith binds us to one another. Through faith we experience ourselves as God's friends and as brothers and sisters in his presence.

To the extent that faith becomes a gratefully tended virtue or competence in us, we will risk everything to bear witness to it in all aspects of our lives. We will nurture the burning wish for all women and men to experience and treasure the light of faith. Faith creates community. Through faith we become the family of God. Faith creates new, healthy, and healing human relations.

In the light of faith, our capacities and our possessions—because they are gifts from the one God—become a binding expression of solidarity. When this solidarity is weakly developed among Christians or is missing entirely, the result is a lack of faith or an extremely defective faith.

Faith cannot be taught as, say, mathematics is taught. Since it is the revelation and gift of the One who is all love, this One wishes to be fruitful in and through love. Authentic faith points always to God.

Faith is a treasure entrusted to the whole Christian world. It promises the salvation of all men and women. The whole Church must commit itself to joyfully professing the virtue of faith, to entering ever more deeply into its mystery, and to credibly proclaiming it. "See how they love one another," says Tertullian. Such faith is then fit to communicate the central contents of Christianity: "God is love. He loves all people."

We can speak of faith as a "theological virtue" only to the degree that we gratefully profess it, and continuously strive to better understand the Good News. Faith is the theological virtue that encourages us to work and pray that our faith may bear fruit in love, justice, and the advancement of peace. We must constantly ask ourselves—and at times this question will haunt us—whether our faith is really effective and fruitful.

A right understanding of why faith is called a theological virtue will constantly challenge us and make us examine our consciences: Why does our faith often strike people as so unattractive? Do the women and men around us really sense that faith is our most precious possession? Do they see clearly that it makes us "fruitful," above all, in love, justice, peacemaking, and dealing responsibly with creation?

7

Hope: Love-Filled Confidence

The goal of God's creation and revelation is the definitive and comprehensive victory of love. How is this virtue of love related to the theological virtue of hope? What makes hope a virtue, nothing less than a theological or divine one?

Hope is a kind of confidence inspired by love. We become bearers of hope when by a sort of "contagion" we stir up in others the confidence that they can draw upon the power of this love to reshape their lives and the world around them.

If we hope and long for thousands of things, and then simply throw in the victory of love for good measure, we are good for nothing. This kind of hope has nothing to do with the theological virtue of hope. The same rule that holds for hope also holds for faith. If we believe in a thousand and one things, and just throw in God for good measure, we have already betrayed and dismissed God in our heart. The theological virtue of hope says that "God alone is enough."

We will achieve a full life when we have full confidence that love will ultimately conquer all. As a result, this sort of confidence will awaken the best powers within us. Such confidence cannot cause us to slack off because it is based on the faith, attested to by God himself, that we may—that we must—work together with him, receptively and responsibly, for the final victory of love.

If Christians think only of saving their own souls, then they have made themselves incapable of the divinely guaranteed hope and confidence that God wishes to be all in all—and ultimately *will* be all in all.

If we live on and in the divinely given and assured hope for the all-embracing kingdom of love and peace, then we will always be concerned with the whole—with the victory of love, of justice, and of peace for everyone.

Only the gift of hope guaranteed by God can transform our many defeats and sufferings into signs of hope. This guarantee takes us to the core of the theological virtue of hope, a virtue rooted above all in the paschal mystery of Christ.

In this paschal mystery, Christ radically transformed a meaningless, cruelly inflicted suffering into an expression of a powerful and reconciling love. He awakens and strengthens hope in the heart of the criminal who, as a sign of contempt, was crucified alongside him: "Today you will be with me in Paradise." In turn, in the heart of the crucified Jesus, the suffering, abandoned thief's cry for help finds its deepest, most resonant echo: "My God, my God, why have you forsaken me?" Christ himself answers this question—a question that torments all of us—not in some theoretical fashion, but with an answer that radically transforms everything:

"Abba, Father, into your hands I commit my spirit." This cry is a true homecoming and victory of love. This final, heartbreaking "Abba" said by Jesus on the cross awakens in us a divinely based confidence, even amid our guilt and distress.

The first Abba-prayer of Jesus on the cross is the all-embracing plea for reconciliation and forgiveness: "Abba, Father, forgive them, they know not what they do." These words, full of powerful confidence, awaken in us a doubled confidence in response: first, that all personal sin and guilt will be forgiven if one enters into the Abba-prayer of Jesus; second, this most intimate prayer obliges and enables us to take part in redemption permanently, to practice healing, reconciling love, and to be always ready to forgive. If we, with God's grace, unreservedly and unconditionally forgive everyone for everything, then we have the divine assurance, backed by God's words and deeds that we have been reconciled, that we have received salvation.

It is clear now that the theological virtue of hope is no idle resource, but a divine challenge enabling us to work together for reconciliation and peace. If anyone finds this virtue of hope passé and irrelevant, then that person has outlived his or her usefulness. Such people are demonstrating the lowest and worst degree of moral incompetence.

There are no lazy virtues. Virtues, and especially the three theological virtues, are a stirring wake-up call; they are the highest kind of competence and the noblest mission.

Several additional but related questions have to be clearly

posed and answered. Are the three theological virtues focused only on the next world? Are they escapist? Do they render us useless for this life on earth? Anyone familiar with Christ and his Gospel knows and has felt in the depths of his or her soul that exactly the opposite is true. Those who confidently say *yes* to the vocation of eternal life have thereby already given the strongest affirmation to their calling here on earth. Those who dream of eternal peace in heaven even as they sow discord or those who make no commitment whatsoever to peace and justice on earth have declared themselves useless for both this time and eternity. Those who sin constantly and irresponsibly against our planet and the life upon it run the greatest risk of making themselves unworthy and incapable of an eternal Paradise. Virtues allow and provide for no alibis.

8

Justice: A Creation of Love

One of the keys to Christian theology is the idea that we cannot make ourselves just in God's eyes through works of the law. This truth leaves no room for cheap excuses. Out of pure, unmerited love, God calls us and leads us forth from the disastrous twinship of sin and injustice. As a result, he has a right to expect that our grateful love will enable us to resist, on all fronts, the forces of destruction and the ruinous entanglements of guilt. Then, empowered by the gift of salvation, we can share in the solidarity of salvation in this earthly life and look forward to everlasting life. In this sense, I say, and our whole faith says, love accepted with gratitude creates justice.

The rich glutton in Luke 16:19-31 who has no room in his heart for the poor Lazarus, and who can spare Lazarus neither attention nor a piece of bread, is barring himself from the kingdom of solidarity in salvation. It is not God who condemns the sinner. It is, rather, the unjust person who has sinned against his or her fellow men and women and who, insofar as possible, turns the earth into a hell, thereby being excluded from salvation and from the kingdom of love.

It is part of the essence of the kingdom of God, a kingdom of love, that a person has to choose. There are only two paths: either the kingdom of solidarity in salvation attained through true justice and love or the domain of perdition with all of its consequences for those who seek it.

Paul uses drastic language to describe the tug and pull of these two domains. Inveterate selfishness, as Paul sees it, takes aim at the spirit, and the spirit fights against inveterate selfishness: "For what the flesh desires is opposed to the Spirit, and what the Spirit desires is opposed to the flesh; for these are opposed to each other" (Gal 5:17). By inveterate selfishness we mean not just wrong-headed and destructive attitudes and the resulting infection of the actions of individuals. Selfishness is at work also in the very structure of modern life, for example, in the terrible fact that the 20 percent of humans inhabiting the Northern Hemisphere consume 80 percent of the nonrenewable resources while emitting 80 percent of the harmful pollutants, and, in the process, damaging our planet and our lives.

If love and justice are really virtues, then this means a wise, indefatigable struggle against the structures of calloused selfishness, and a constant striving for healthy relationships and healing structures. Where Christians forget or neglect these facts, we need not be surprised that, consequently, some think that virtue has had it. Perhaps virtue has merely gone into retirement, leaving the unselfish to pay the high price of maintaining it.

If virtue is to be rehabilitated, we must pitilessly unmask

every form of hypocrisy. There can be no doubt left about the Christian virtues. They are burningly relevant here and now, but they cannot be had on the cheap.

The Christian virtues confront us with a radical challenge. A brief description should suffice to suggest just *how* radical virtue is and how necessary it is to make an unconditionally clear option for good. Redeemed love can never accept the treatment of women as inferior to men either in private life (marriage, the family, relationships) or in society or in the Church. The marginalization of the physically impaired, refugees, or those who have in one way or another come to grief so that the powerful can become more powerful, the rich can become richer, and the well-placed can find even cushier places is a colossal injustice. It is unfair not only of those who have created such marginalization and who directly profit from it but also unfair of those who refuse to lift a finger to produce a more just and more humane social order.

If we want to have a share in the Beatitudes, then we must also make a radical commitment to the demands that they make and to keep pressing forward in the direction that they lead. We must avoid giving our allegiance to a watering down of virtue, a degradation that only deforms and discredits it.

If we wish to experience and have others experience the power of virtue to spread blessings and bliss, then we have to make radical decisions. At the very least, we have to decide clearly the direction in which we want to go, and day by day take the steps in that direction that are possible here and now. Then no one can accuse us Christians of having long since sent the highest Christian virtues into retirement without even paying them a pension.

The future of the ecumenical movement, which is a great grace, will also depend on how well the virtue of justice is lived by the world's Christians. The ecumenical movement will succeed only to the extent that all churches and church authorities commit themselves wholeheartedly to work for peace, justice, and ecological responsibility. Those who dodge these issues out of laziness or even for reasons of prestige have already betrayed their honor and credibility.

9

Prudence:
The Vigilant Eye of Love

In Hellenistic and Roman culture, prudence was considered one of the cardinal virtues. Over the centuries since, however, it has undergone a great deal of narrowing and distortion.

In the great Chinese tradition, especially in Confucianism, prudence is not classified as a cardinal virtue. Instead, Confucius says that the four precious gifts of the Tao (heaven) are goodness of heart, politeness (an expression of goodness of heart), public-spiritedness, and justice. Here prudence is seen as an expression of goodness of heart. It is fully a virtue and serves to build up a healthy society. For this reason, I think that prudence should probably best be understood as the vigilant eye of love—an eye that can estimate what love demands and what authentically expresses love, or what adulterates it.

The dangerous opposite of prudence is cunning, a cunning that tries to put everything to work for the selfish interests of the individual and the group. The Italians speak, significantly, of *sacro egoismo*. Sometimes, in their private lives, people steer clear of any exploitation of their neighbor only to pay a high tax to the egoism of the group. The sanctification of group egoism is a horrible caricature of the whole domain of the holy and the good.

"My country, my company, my group: right or wrong." Nothing else matters except the homeland, the group, or corporate interests. Humanity can thank this stupid collective egoism for all kinds of senseless wars and frightful criminal conspiracies. Group egoism has produced and supported untold cunning in the development of its structures and behavior patterns. The genuine virtue of prudence, together with the virtue of bravery, is needed to strip away the veil from all these pious frauds and reveal them in all their naked crudity.

Only the genuine virtue of prudence—the vigilant eye of love and salvific solidarity—will not allow itself to be subverted. It is only the love that comes from it, and leads back to God, that can successfully take up the struggle against lies and hypocrisy. If the cunning that is alien to God succeeds, then prudence is by its very nature ready to pay any price—and sometimes it is a high one—in the service of God. There are no virtues that are not costly. Real prudence cannot be found in the marketplace of utilitarianism or of cut-rate practicality.

Only the steadfast who are prepared to pay the price for the coming of the kingdom of love, peace, and justice will be able to recognize the best interests of the kingdom. Only the brave, the vigilant, the bright-eyed, who are ready for martyrdom, possess this clear-eyed view of love that we call prudence.

The goal of wisdom and love is healthy and healing human relationships and helpful and liberating social and Church structures. Prudence is a vehicle for exploring the ways and means to achieve these ends. For example, social, political, or even church structures with too many controls and too high a level of mistrust are pathological insofar as they block trusting and promising relationships. No matter how cleverly such structures may be organized, however well they may be hidden behind a pious front, they are not the expression of either wisdom or prudence. These misleading structures fail because they do not serve the cause of love, peace, and justice, nor do they foster healthy, healing human relations.

According to the Gospel, true prudence goes hand in hand with the "simplicity of doves." It absolutely requires the unequivocal clarity of the peaceable and of peacemakers. But simplicity certainly does not mean naiveté or blindness to every risk. Simplicity does, however, call for the courage to expose oneself to some serious dangers while acting on behalf of love, and while meeting one's commitment to love, justice, and peace.

Prudence must also provide protection as far as possible against everything that harms the kingdom of love. But something is awry if prudence is seen as merely trying to avoid trouble or sacrifice. In this instance, meditate on the careerists in society or the Church, the ambitious people who deftly lay every word and action on the scales to see if it is to their advantage or to see if it promotes their own interests. When prudence breaks down in this way, no room is left for wisdom and for true love.

10

COURAGE: A GIFT OF LOVE

Love gives us more than the clear, vigilant eye that catches sight of the paths of love and exposes the dead ends. It also grants us the virtue of courage or *strength of soul*.

Loves makes us inwardly strong. This is the strength that steadily and unswervingly draws upon the driving force and "carrying capacity" of brave, vigilant love. Love is the most intimate and powerful force of all. It creates strength of soul devoted to everything that serves love and that demands to be defended against the threats to love. As Paul says, "[Love] bears all things" and "endures all things" (1 Cor 13:7).

Love's strength of soul is proclaimed and demonstrated from the pulpit of the cross. There we see the proof that love is as strong as death. As he hangs on the cross, Jesus thinks of himself only so he can surrender completely to the Father and seek his honor. He is all love and strength of soul for us, for all those who stand beneath the cross and look up to him. Jesus' strength of soul is expressed in the prayer: "Not my will but yours be done" (Lk 22:42).

His strong-souled love has a sharp eye for the afflicted.

He, the Man of Sorrows, comforts the weeping women and mothers. He turns in prayer to us sinners, to all sinners: "Father, forgive them!" With wonderfully expressive love, he turns to all outcasts in the person of the thief: "Today you will be with me in Paradise" (Lk 23:43). The strong love of Jesus is the single flame in which love for the Father and for us human beings meets and fuses.

The high point of Jesus' love unto death on the cross is his love of his enemies. His love is stronger than hatred, than all hostility. Here we see clearly the meaning of love of one's enemies and of reconciling love. This is the love for which his heart beats till the last.

The strength of Jesus' love is matched by his utmost daring. In a figurative yet concrete sense, we can call the creation of humans—with their fragile freedom that can even deny its origins—an unheard-of, bold, and daring decision prompted by the strongest love. This boldness is exceeded only by the work of redemption. There the Word of God takes on the form of a slave, in order to lure humanity onto the true path of life and to bring them to a boundless love. What greater boldness of love could be imagined than the Way of the Cross trodden by the nonviolent Son and Servant of God?

The responsive love of human beings should have in it something of this boldness of the divine yet human love of Jesus. In fact, the lives of the saints are a constantly renewed epic tale of strong-hearted and bold-spirited love. And aren't there millions of Christians and adherents of other religions as well who have distinguished themselves by the power of their love of neighbor and by the strength of love that flows from their love of God? Tireless patience in peacemaking amid every conceivable risk testifies to love's greatness and its strength.

Strength of soul in suffering is in no way inferior to strength of soul in deeds of daring love. A million times over the martyrs have hymned this supreme strength. Without lamenting or hesitating, they went to their deaths to testify to their faith and love. For all the talk about weak women, women were in no way inferior to strong-souled men in their endurance of torture on the way to martyrdom.

We can never admire enough the strength of soul of the women and mothers who, despite all their disappointments, kept the bonds of conjugal and motherly love intact. Again and again we ask this question: Where do they or did they get this power, this perseverance? The answer must go something like this: from the strength of selfless, redeemed and redeeming love.

In our daily prayer, "…and lead us not into temptation," we ask to be spared trials that would exceed our strength. But behind this there always stands the brave request that God may increase love in us so greatly that we can, in cooperation with his grace, prove ourselves strong, even in difficult trials. No prayer is more important than this one: "Lord, increase your love in us!"

11

MODERATION: MEASURING by Love's STANDARD

Unless we bring some standards of evaluation to all our desires and to our whole lifestyle, we can never grow in the love of God and our neighbor. These standards must be above and beyond all merely human standards of measurement.

It is truly worthwhile, if we wish to keep a tight rein on ourselves, to resist all unnecessary desires. That way we gather our energies for loving. Indeed, we constantly practice loving, if and to the extent that our moderation and renunciation flow from love and aim toward the greater love in each case.

The love that wants to grow in us, the love that God himself wishes to intensify in us, expresses itself in many guises and gives us many reasons to practice the virtue of moderation. Jesus' speech in Matthew 25 about the Last Judgment points us toward a whole series of urgent situations that radically test the strength and genuineness of our love.

"I was hungry and you gave me food," says Jesus. If we

look upon the hungry with eyes of faith, then we see that it is Jesus himself who asks for sustenance. In this light, if love is really setting the standards, may we eat and drink beyond our needs in the face of this request? Without doing ourselves the least harm, we could give up a great deal of luxury in the way we live.

"I was homeless," says the Lord. Can we Christians then allow ourselves deluxe houses and apartments, when thousands, even millions, of people are either homeless or wretchedly housed? Let us use the ballot to force politicians to do more to guarantee everyone, including political refugees, more humane living conditions. We cannot just say that we lack the means, as long as boundless luxury flourishes side by side with the misery of the homeless.

"I was naked and you clothed me," says Jesus. How many unnecessary articles of clothing fill our closets? How can a Christian, for whom love sets all standards and ranks highest in the scale of values, show contempt for people in rags by parading around dressed to the nines? It is not necessary to actually say words of contempt in order to degrade the poor; we can say words of contempt through our behavior.

"I was sick and you visited me," says Jesus. If all Christians, or at least many Christians, were to recognize the suffering Christ in the sick, then many sick and old would not have to live alone and in neglect. So those who prize love above all will also look beyond the narrow boundaries of their own country and generously contribute to the care of the sick and suffering throughout the world. When funds are being raised to alleviate the misery of people everywhere, do we sincerely measure the situation by the only valid standard: Christ's love for us and the grace of faith?

Some years ago in the United States, I met several nuns who belonged to the House of Prayer movement. After retiring as college teachers, these women devoted most of their energies to caring for those in prisons and penitentiaries. As they saw it, visits to the Blessed Sacrament would no longer be authentic if they were not also visiting and encouraging the men and women in prison (Mt 25:36).

More of this sort of thing is going on all over the world than some of us imagine. But it is far from being enough. Evidently we do not realize that love, which is the key to everything, wants to set the standards for the works of corporal and spiritual mercy. In particular, love sets the specific standard appropriate for us. Even if we did come to some weak realization, we would no doubt keep discovering that we can still do much more than we are doing now. We should never follow in the footsteps of stingy millionaires who continually calculate how to increase their assets or how to make a further killing on the stock market. Shouldn't we try, instead, to discover how generosity and the love of Christ could grow in us in a much more careful and imaginative way?

In this context, let us again reflect on the true meaning of prayer: "Lord, increase faith in us, kindle love in us!" Such prayer will keep leading us back to self-scrutiny. In the face of the depth and breadth of the love of Jesus bears for us miserable creatures, let us ask in particular whether our love passes the test of dealing with those who cannot even begin to pay us back.

It is bad for us when we do want to practice moderation but in the process we completely lose sight of the true standard: the love with which Christ loves us and the chances he gives us to confirm this love by our offering it to those who need our help. In their concern for false moderation, many Christians are all too self-satisfied. We all can and should make a much greater effort to increase our practice of love. And, just realizing that the virtue of moderation sets the guidelines for love is revolutionary. How much richer in love might not we all become!

12

Compassion: The Image of God's Love

L ove is compassionate. This is a core principle and a high point of Christian faith and Christian teaching on the virtues. Still further, compassion is a key to the Christian notion of perfection and even a mirror of the image of God.

The Sermon on the Mount identifies compassion with perfection. The version of the statement found in Matthew 5:48 "You, therefore, must be perfect, as your heavenly Father is perfect" is given in Luke as "Be merciful, just as your Father is merciful" (Lk 6:36). In so doing, Luke is only clarifying and putting beyond dispute a point made in Matthew's Gospel.

The demand "to be perfect, as your heavenly Father is perfect" is illustrated by the powerful stress on Jesus' compassion: "Love your enemies and pray for those who persecute you, so that you may be sons of your Father who is in heaven; for he makes his sun rise on the evil and on the good, and sends rain on the just and on the unjust" (Mt

5:44–45). Here we see with unmatched clarity the characteristic feature of both Christianity's image of God and its teaching on virtue. In contrast, the god of Greek and Roman philosophers sits impassively on his throne, looking down on human beings, untroubled by the passion of sympathy. Hence, the typical Greek and Roman philosophers and their disciples would be untouched by the suffering of others.

The cross unmistakably proclaims compassion, the utterly compassionate love of God. That is what spells out the Christian vision of love as compassionate. And that is not something added on or accidental; it comes from the center and points toward the summit. The Christian peak experience is always bound up with God's compassion and with the compassion of his true sons and daughters.

Of course, there is no way to miss the fact that this quintessentially Christian virtue comes at a high price. How dearly we cost God—we who have been redeemed at great expense. There is no way we can seriously and truthfully profess our faith in the God of love, in the Father of our Lord Jesus Christ, without also professing his compassion. Practically speaking, this means radically taking upon ourselves the duty of compassionate love.

Compassion implies the most intimate sympathy with people who are suffering, despised, and marginalized. Harsh judgments of others by any "paragon of virtue" who invokes God, even the God our Lord Jesus Christ, reveal total shamelessness.

God's compassionate, healing, and liberating love has

been unsurpassably portrayed in the parable of the Prodigal Son (Lk 15:11–32). In his misery, the son turns to his father, who then prepares a festive banquet to welcome him home. The Father invites us all to take part in the feast of compassionate love. The virtue of Christian compassion flourishes wherever Christians honestly confront and express the power of this parable. Wherever compassion is missing, "works of righteousness" are poisoned.

The virtue of compassion, when faithfully put into practice, comes at a high price. In the face of the suffering of heartlessly despised people, the compassionate person is shaken by sympathy and enlists to do something for them. True sympathy urges us to action. Active sympathy makes it clear that we are on the way to worshiping God as the supremely compassionate one and honoring him in a real-life fashion.

Without compassion, both zeal for the law and zeal for piety lose their credibility. That is the point of the parable of the Good Samaritan (Lk 10:29–37). Anyone who thinks that his piety is validated by mystical peak-experiences, but passes by his neighbor's bitter need, is like the priest and Levite who deliberately ignore the distress of their brutalized fellow Jew. Every intimate experience of God, every authentic spiritual consolation, urges us to effective compassion. The grateful signs of divine grace impel us from within to show sympathy and active compassion.

The divine cost of compassion is infinitely high: the Incarnation of the Word of God, the suffering and dying of the Savior on the cross, was fashioned by human hardheartedness and bitter zeal for the law. Raising our eyes in gratitude to the cross teaches us to give thanks through deeply felt sympathy and through active compassion—and not just in rare, exceptional cases—but in the whole way we shape our lives and in all our human relationships.

Our little mortifications and ascetical exercises have value to the extent that they serve to train us in active compassion and self-denial that this compassion inevitably calls for. It is worthwhile to read the Bible through, paying special attention to the revelations of divine compassion and to the corresponding call to redeemed and compassionate love. The tears we shed at the sight of the crucified Jesus must spur us on to honor in our existence the divine Redeemer in all the downtrodden, marginalized, and bitterly suffering people in the world.

12

Creative Fidelity: A Mark of True Love

True love for God, and all love that comes from God, is marked by creative fidelity. The virtue of creative fidelity is ever alert. It is founded on the totality of divine revelation. It is faithfully attentive to the signs of the times. It is marked by mutual care for discernment of the spirits and empathetic consideration for latecomers.

The virtue of creative fidelity is built on the concepts of creative conscience and creative freedom. Some Church leaders still warn against such ideas. They are obviously afraid of disorder. They worry that morality could get out of control.

Core moral concepts, such as freedom, conscience, obedience, and fidelity, can have very different meanings and importance. These differing meanings depend on if our concern is with conformity, fulfilling norms, and subordination, or instead if our focus is radical thinking infused with the spirit of God blowing as it wills and marked by grown-up, freely affirmed responsibility. People are afraid of differences and of the brave spirit of initiative. These crucial differences are connected to one's personal image of God.

God, our Creator, has in his sovereign freedom set in motion a tension-filled path of development. Along with regular patterns of order, scientists find clear but indeterminate factors that, over the course of billions of years, have played an enormous role. From explosive chaos arises new synthesis. Other unknowable factors play as yet undreamed-of roles. For all the splendor of nature's laws, God's creation always has surprises in store for us. Deeper, more penetrating insight into this continuous dynamic leaves us breathless.

Above all this, God has obviously set a grand history of freedom in motion, in which humans can act in a way that is either creative or that is hostile to freedom and hence destructive. One thing we do know: God's creation, including the human race, will never slip out of his hands.

Teilhard de Chardin (1881–1955), with his astonishing scientific knowledge and breadth of vision, discovered new dimensions of historic interpretation, including the history of freedom. But Church leaders found his visions and suggestive ideas just as upsetting and unacceptable as those of Galileo. It is no wonder that during his lifetime he barely managed to publish anything.

With the Second Vatican Council, a powerful current swept through the life of the Church, affecting theology as well as views of science. The core and central concern of the movement set in motion by the Second Vatican Council was creative fidelity. To no one's surprise, Catholic fundamentalism felt it had been wounded and lashed back. Fundamentalists, of whatever stripe, insist on doctrines and norms, on clearly defined customs and traditions that can be controlled from above. One could hardly find a better example of misunderstood fidelity than the famous dispute over the Chinese rites in the eighteenth century. The upshot of this dispute was that not only did the Chinese have to celebrate Mass in Latin, but they were told to be loyal and "keep the faith" by sticking primarily to Western and Latin abstractions.

Nowadays, creative fidelity expresses itself in terms such as inculturation, incarnational theology, and so forth. The point has to be made as emphatically as possible: "creative fidelity" is far more demanding than mechanical fidelity that is controlled down to the tiniest detail. The transition from the paradigm of obedience to the virtue of responsibility and the responsible awareness of the adult Christian can sometimes be a painful and turbulent process. The same thing is true of the transition from a static understanding of fidelity to creative fidelity.

One sometime hears the argument that the pace of history has speeded up as never before and that those who cling to a static and authoritarian fidelity are simply going to be steamrollered. Important as this point is, there is more to it than mere ascendancy or descendency.

Creative fidelity, equipped with alertness to the signs of the times, with care for the discernment of the spirits and empathetic consideration for latecomers, has its foundation in the totality of divine revelation. Practicing the virtue of creative fidelity is very demanding. It presupposes and demands a deep, continuously growing interiorization of divine revelation. In the whole process of interpretation, it insists on special attentiveness and continuity in fruitful tension with the need to keep a sharp lookout for novelty both now and for the coming generation.

A typical counter-model of creative fidelity is the group of fundamentalists gathered around Bishop Marcel Lefebvre. Had they gotten their way and pushed through their harsh agenda, the Church would have very quickly become a museum. However, the Church would no longer be the salvific community of the wandering people of God. The heavy stress on the latter in the Church's document *Lumen gentium* is an important reference to the paradigm of "creative fidelity."

We can say a complete and real-life *yes* to this model only if we pay the closest attention to the dogma of the Holy Spirit, and study it intently. Creative fidelity is a turning away from minimalism, a rejection of a spare rigidity that is oriented almost exclusively to the negative commandments. The more one internalizes the Beatitudes and the whole Sermon on the Mount, the more creative fidelity flourishes. The question no longer is, Where exactly is the boundary line between mortal sin and venial sin? Instead the life-and-death question for creative freedom is, How can I repay the Lord for all that he has done for me? The foundation here is constituted by the so-called eschatological virtues, the dynamic virtues of salvation history: gratitude, through which the fruitfulness of the past is continually renewed, turning to the here and now in wakefulness, readiness, and communal struggle for the gift of discernment. In this way, one opens up creatively to the hour of grace and moves forward in hope and responsibility into the future.

Only if we grow in devoted solidarity and creative fidelity will we become the salt and leaven of history. In other words, fidelity becomes a powerful historical force. Thanks to creative fidelity we are the people of God, ready for the Exodus and ever-new departures.

PART THREE

14

The Virtue of Gratitude

People who possess the virtue of gratitude are innerly rich. They not only know how richly they have been blessed, but continuously remember that all good things come from God. This remembrance is the most precious and blessed feature of the virtue of gratitude.

In the hard times in Germany after World War II, I met three women who were refugees. They were the incarnation of the "deserving poor." Since at the moment I myself had nothing at all, I turned to a rich devout Catholic whom I knew: "Please help generously!" I pleaded. To which he promptly answered: "Why me? So far nobody's given *me* anything." I was horrified, and told him: "You surely are the poorest man of all. Obviously you haven't yet discovered that everything you own is a gift from God. Is God 'nobody' to you?" He took a deep breath and opened his wallet.

The ingrate is cold-hearted, lonely, and, despite his self-satisfaction, basically unhappy. The miser is inwardly impoverished, empty, and dried up.

On the other hand, the more thankful a person is, the

richer he or she is within. Such people know they are continuously being blessed with gifts. They have an intuition that God is giving himself to them. The thoroughly grateful person is either already a profound believer or living the "analogy of faith"—a phrase I prefer to Karl Rahner's "anonymous Christians." Faith is a thankful reception of the love of God as it reveals itself to us.

Spouses who prize each other as a gift discover together their best capacities. What happiness when the children sense that their parents and siblings see them as gifts from God, as in the names Dorothy and Theodore (both meaning gift of God).

Gratitude makes us sensitive and sharp-eyed. It is creative. People bound together by gratitude are always discovering and awakening abundant sources of strength.

Faith in God is of an altogether different type among grateful people than is faith among the ungrateful. The thankless person may subscribe to all the Church's dogmas, but he or she never experiences the essential, blissful quality of faith. For grateful people, faith increasingly becomes a festive way of accepting the love of God as it gives and reveals itself. Ungrateful people are at the bottom, always sullen, always inclined to pity themselves for having gotten the worst of it. They cannot ever be really satisfied and happy either with themselves or with others.

All talk about love where there is no mention of gratitude is on the wrong track. Apparent love coming from an ingrate misses the mark, because it isn't meant for the "beloved" in and for the beloved's self. On the other hand, those who live with grateful people realize that they aren't just accepted, but honored and prized.

Thankful people store up in their grateful memory all the good experiences of the past. And in this way, the richness of the past, of tradition, and the whole variety of positive experiences, become a treasure, a source of energy for the here and now. Gratitude is a permanently open channel through which all good things from the past and everything that the present offers become living and fruitful.

Am I exaggerating when I claim that the grace of God really flows our way only to the extent that the channel of gratitude is open? Through ingratitude, humans keep losing again and again the paradise of happy mutual relations. The actual beauty and preciousness of all earthly goods remains hidden to the ingrate, while it richly waters the garden of the thankful.

God's grace is characterized by its literal gratuitousness—by the fact that it is a gift that sends us back to the original source of love. Even under momentarily adverse circumstances, grateful people are not full of misery, for they still have a thousand reasons for thanking God. And this means that the experience of gratuitousness stamps even the trials we are undergoing right now with the sign of redemption.

When I gratefully accept the help and encouragement of thankful people, I don't feel humiliated; on the contrary, I feel honored and cheered up. Gratitude makes Christians capable of the Eucharist (whose literal meaning is "thanksgiving"). According to the measure of their gratitude, they find the infinite riches of God's saving deeds flowing to them afresh. They let themselves be swept up into the fruitful story of divine love and of human love responding to it.

Thanklessness is a sort of antechamber to hell. Gratitude is an antechamber to heaven, a preparation for entering the eternal song of praise of God's goodness. Every act of gratitude, above all, the careful cultivation of the virtue of thankfulness, shapes the fabric of the grace of perseverance in the good.

15

Alertness: A Response to the Grace of Gratitude

For thankful persons, every moment can become a moment of grace, or *kairos*. They know that they have been made a part of salvation history in both a receptive and in a cooperative way. That is why they are vigilant. They are on the right wavelength; they have a feel for the opportunities of the here and now. In their encounters with their fellow men and women, including those who personally need their help, their thankful faith hears the cry, the voice of Jesus, and senses his glance.

On the other hand, proud paragons of virtue become entangled in the grid of their virtues. Vigilant Christians, by contrast, live with complete intensity in salvation history; they are always in the here and now, and they discover what the hour offers and demands from them. Truly vigilant people see that even thorny moments contain more than trouble and danger. They often discover surprisingly valuable opportunities where others find nothing but reasons for lamentation.

The ingrate is forever yoked to the ifs and buts, while

grateful people have said good-bye forever to conditional statements. Their defining motto is, Here I am, Lord. Call me. What do you want from me, Lord?

Of course, vigilance also implies attentiveness. Attentive people do not stumble into every ditch. But their avoidance of stumbling blocks occurs, as it were, incidentally, through their wakeful, ready reply of *yes* to positive possibilities.

The wise virgins in Matthew 25:1–13 wait for the coming of the Lord with their lamps lit. And the oil of love and readiness will not fail. To me this means, among other things, that we should not have any false self-confidence. We should always "watch and pray." Even vigilance, the wide-awake eye for present opportunities to do good, is all grace. And we have to keep telling ourselves this over and over again, saying it out loud in the presence of God and praying: "Don't let us wander into meaningless temptations!"

Vigilance is not just a private virtue. If many of us Christians are fully alert to the opportunity and the call of the moment, then a Christian world will emerge ready to take on its responsibility in salvation history.

In this instance, I am always assaulted by the nightmare of moralists who are forever hammering into our heads their absolutisms, commands, and prohibitions detached from time and space. With all their prohibitions against this or that, they distract the eyes of the travelers so that they risk losing their way and completely missing the beauty all around them.

The decision by the commission charged with drawing

up the pastoral constitution, "The Church in Today's World," to address all the important problems with a special focus on the signs of the times was crucial for Vatican II's renewal of the Church. We should not overlook the fact that the Council was acting quite deliberately, and in particular following the spirit of Pope John XXIII, when it looked first and foremost to the encouraging signs of the times, the signs of God's presence. By contrast, anticonciliar fundamentalists and pessimists lament the opportunities of the moment and sit impassive in the face of the encouraging signs of God's activity in history.

The vigilance of the Church as a whole builds on the vigilance of individuals and communities. Above all, the Church needs priests, woman pastoral caregivers, and bishops who are keenly aware of the positive opportunities and whose character is stamped by the Paraclete, the Holy Spirit, the Comforter. Priests and bishops who are pessimists and blind to positive opportunities have a contagious effect on those around them. It would be a great advance for the Church's mission if all those priests and bishops whose thinking is out of touch with the times would acknowledge that they are a source of infection and would seek help.

Rootedness in the here and now, the dynamic view of history as the salvation story and a dedication to pastoral care exposes the alienating attempt to enforce uniformity in language, liturgy, and theology. Such regimentation inevitably leads to theological and ecclesiastical colonialism. Standardization in thought, speech, and action can operate only out of a narrow position, with contempt for others and otherness. Remember that God works through complex harmonies, not monotony.

All these temptations will surely be overcome when the whole body of the Church's theology and praxis gives the appropriate attention to the biblical, salvation-history virtues, especially the virtue of alertness to the here and now, and draws practical conclusions from them.

16

The Virtue of Discernment

The gift of discernment or, more fully, the discernment of spirits, is a specifically Christian virtue. It is frequently mentioned in the New Testament. In the final analysis, it is thought of less as a virtuous human activity than as a gift of the Holy Spirit. As we let ourselves be guided by the Spirit of God and serve him with a pure heart and an unselfish intention, we learn to distinguish between what comes from and leads to God—and what can promote the coming of God's Kingdom—from what can become a stumbling block.

Discernment is, above all, a virtue of salvation history. The more ardently we pray and long for the coming of the Kingdom of God, the more we develop a sharp eye for what hastens or impedes it. Discernment unfolds in responsible attentiveness to the here and now. It naturally also includes attentiveness to the future, a future that we approach through seizing the present moment.

This virtue of discernment presupposes the other salvation-history virtues, above all, vigilance and readiness. The more vigilant we are and the readier we are to seek the will of God in all things and to serve the coming of the Kingdom here and now, the more clearly we see and grasp the opportunity of the present moment.

The heart of discernment is found in vigilance and a sharp eye for the pregnant possibilities of salvation, together with attentiveness to dangerous obstacles. If we are open to the workings of the Holy Spirit, we will increasingly be given the gift of discerning the difference between holy and unholy love.

Instead of the virtue of discernment, we can also speak of the virtue of criticism. The word *criticism* comes from the Greek word *krinein,* meaning "to judge" or "to discern." Not just individuals but also communities and the Church as a whole have to cultivate the virtue of criticism and restore it to its proper place. This restoration will happen if we are willing to let ourselves be challenged by prophetic-critical men and women. A Church institution that not only does not heed the prophets, but persecutes them, has thereby dangerously slammed the door on the virtue of criticism.

If, in addition, critical spirits are attractive personal models, then the chances are good that they will help in the formation of the virtue of discernment. By contrast, embittered critics and petty faultfinders are good for nothing, least of all for fostering the spirit of solidarity that strives for an evermore mature and accurate discernment.

In order to ripen, the virtue of criticism needs encouragement, which means, among other things, that parents and educators have to take seriously the nagging "Why this?"

and "Why that?" of children and teenagers. A common reaction of authority figures, "Don't ask, just do it" can have catastrophic results: either it leads to uncritical docility or to a rebellious spirit.

It is no less devastating for the cultivation of the spirit of discernment when people in authority surround themselves with yeasayers. When yeasayers dominate the domain of the Church, a quiet, but often cunning, revolt against the virtue of discernment takes place. We all know moralists who damned everything within the purview of the sixth commandment as an intrinsically serious sin. Yet, strangely enough, many of them didn't have a word to say about the sins of the authoritarians in the Church who geared everything to the "culture" of submissiveness and to the promotion of those whose eager response is always *Yes*. This masturbatory style of leadership is infinitely and essentially worse and more dangerous than the much-damned sins against purity.

We live in a time of radical change. The course of history has quickened as never before. Stubborn clinging to human traditions and dogmatic formulations have caused parts of the Church to become spiritually sterile and reactionary. History is rapidly leaving these parts of the Church behind in the dust.

Both the history of Israel, as recorded in the Old Testament, and the story of Jesus and his true disciples as told in the New Testament, show us with unmistakable clarity that it is precisely the powerful religious leaders who insist on their power by constantly invoking God who are always at the ready, with daggers drawn against the prophets. The history of murder of the prophets by kings and governors, culminating in the murder of the "prophet" Jesus, reveals not just a failure of discernment, but a blind and callous suppression of the virtue of criticism.

The virtue of discernment has a particularly close association with the "signs of the times." One of Jesus' harshest comments on the religious leaders of Israel was: "You know how to interpret the appearance of the sky, but you cannot interpret the signs of the times" (Mt 16:3).

The pastoral constitution *Gaudium et spes* of Vatican II has as its recurrent theme alertness to the signs of the times and to the effort to practice discernment. Before all else, this document speaks continuously and emphatically about the encouraging signs of God's presence. Only thereafter does it voice its opposition to the more calamitous signs of the times. The pessimists are always inclined to see first and foremost—and often nothing but—the disturbing signs of the times, and to complain about just how bad they are. In so doing they have already denied the virtue of discernment. They have affirmed their own blindness.

It also amounts to an attack on God's honor when Church leaders stress the victories of evil in their time, and only then concede in a footnote that some good things are taking place as well. I once found myself urgently advising a clergyman of this sort: "Chase the devil into the corner and leave him there. But, above all, give God the glory." Those who, on principle, always heed with gratitude the encouraging signs of the times can also confront with courage and purposefulness the evil forces at work in our world.

In this age, with its unprecedented opportunities, vigilant Christians realize that they are challenged to live at one with the Lord of history. To do this, it is helpful to strive together for discernment and to cultivate continuously the virtue of criticism. This means, of course, that you and I and all of us have to be receptive to criticism when it comes our way.

Never before has the readiness to change our way of thinking been so necessary for salvific learning as it is today. In some areas, we have to affirm the provisory nature of our situation in order to arrive by gradual stages at a clearer view. Clinging to old formulations and traditions and, no less, the tendency to premature assertions, goes against the virtue of discernment. On this point, however, we should realize that, in our historical moment of exodus, brave steps forward are more in tune with salvation than stubbornly looking back like Lot's wife.

As an old man, let me add that the world and the Church are well advised to prize the wisdom of the old. Still, as life expectancy keeps increasing, this much must be said: Those old priests and prelates who refuse to make way for the young have lost their corner on the market for wisdom.

17

Perseverance

By perseverance I mean the same thing as "staying power." The concept of perseverance is related to what has been said previously about creative fidelity. But it also includes important dimensions of the virtue of strength of spirit. Staying power often requires a high degree of courage. But, as a virtue, it is decisively different from merely a stubborn clinging to the old. There are even forms of perseverance that amount to running in place.

A good general cannot simply carry out a preestablished plan. He does need to make plans, but, equally, he needs constant readiness to respond to new, unexpected situations. The same thing holds true for entrepreneurs and politicians: they are expected to be reliable, but at the same time always alert in the face of new situations.

Staying power or perseverance points to inner sources of energy and strong determination to live a good and moral life dedicated to God. Such a decision can hold up only if it is continually deepened and made more certain.

As Christians, we pray unceasingly for the grace of final perseverance "until death." But we must realize that this final perseverance still implies a readiness to change. Final perseverance absolutely requires continuous preparedness to repent: not just a change of direction, but a radical reorientation and mobilization of all our energies.

Talk about staying power reminds us that our fidelity is always being put to the test and is exposed to doubt and temptation. In the course of our lives, we have to be conscious of the fact that obstacles can suddenly get in our way. We can be tempted both from without and within, and the moment of temptation is precisely the point at which our staying power is called upon most deeply.

Perseverance is not just a matter of warning signs. On the contrary, we will stay the course only if we try always to make the most of the gifts of the moment, keeping our eyes fixed on the goal. Thus, our staying power can and must grow amid all our difficulties. It is always being challenged anew.

The marathoner symbolizes a number of elements involved in the concept of perseverance. He or she breathes deeply and regularly throughout the race. He or she needs oxygen. Staying power lives on in the breath of trust in God, continuously renewed through prayer. He or she needs the deep breath of love, the élan of enthusiasm and, no less, the stimulus of noble competition. We run with one another and learn from one another.

Those who open themselves to the grace of staying power and constantly pray for it can say with the Apostle to the Gentiles: "I can do all things through him who strengthens me" (Phil 4:13).

Perseverance is not just a matter for the individual. It is a matter for the community and calls for solidarity, mutual support, and encouragement. This virtue is not least of all an individual grace; it is an offer to the Christian community, as the Book of Revelation powerfully puts it.

The first Christians were supposed to have expected the imminent return of Christ. It is this anticipation and constant expectation of the return of the Lord that marks the Christian community's view of his ultimate Second Coming, or *parousia*. This hopeful anticipation is a model of the staying power that must be a mark of all Christians in times of trial and in the struggle against the symptoms of fatigue. The early Christians, even as have modern Christians, experienced tests of their perseverance. Toward the end of the first century, Christians had to go through a difficult shift from a proximate expectation to an ongoing expectation of Christ's Second Coming. Only the innermost power of their faith and perseverance enabled them to live such readiness for transformation and to be open to such a demanding grace.

We can find an analogy to this shift in present-day economic life. If modern entrepreneurs were to misunderstand staying power as a stubborn clinging to outdated methods and simply grit their teeth to get through hard times, they would soon find themselves derailed. Readiness to undergo transformation is a prerequisite to staying on the track of faith and virtues. This perseverance is demanding but noble. It is a burning inner energy that requires the sure compass of love and shared responsibility.

18

LIVING on an Advance of TRUST

Living comprehensively and consciously on the basis of a divine advance of trust has a significant meaning for the whole of Christian life. Theological tradition speaks of the grace that comes before, or *gratia praeveniens*. I have tried to convey the deeper implications of this term by calling it "God's advance of trust."

In a further and more fundamental sense, the workings of grace and God's whole plan of salvation are basic features of his anticipation. This anticipation is an overwhelming advance of trust, at which we can never be sufficiently amazed and for which we can never be sufficiently thankful. The fact that God endows us with freedom and releases us into freedom is an unheard-of act of daring. God knows that creatures can misuse this noble gift by disobedience even to the point of rebellion. Nevertheless, God takes the chance with us, with me, with you. In this act we find the foundational and all-embracing advance of trust. Each one of our sins and, above all, our serious sins, are a bitter disappointment in the face of such a divine advance preparation.

Many traditional theologians use the term *gratia prae-*

veniens only to describe the grace that God gives to the sinner. Once again, God takes the first step. He stretches out his hand to snatch up the sinner who is caught again in sin. He enables sinners to make a fresh start. We cannot ever be astonished enough at this. Astonishment and thanks are the first appropriate responses when grappling with the significance of this healing and liberating grace. But these responses are by no means enough.

God expects and wants us to make this anticipatory action a basic feature of our mutual relationships. God's advance of trust, thanks to which we can live and rise up and bear fruit, is the model that obligates us in our own interpersonal relations. Those relationships become healthy and healing to the extent that we keep giving—not just once, but seven times seven—the vitally necessary advance of trust to each other. And we have to do this not in a lofty manner but, humbly, in view of the divine advance of trust on which *we* live.

This persevering advance is what makes human life together, especially in the family, work out successfully. It keeps building and rebuilding bridges. Its opposite, bitter distrust, has catastrophic consequences. When parents keep communicating to their children the message that "There's not much good to be looked for from you" or "You'll never amount to anything," that judgment causes a dangerous discouragement and even a menace to the child's freedom to do good.

In their defiant years, teenagers sometimes express—in a

somewhat unfathomable fashion—the longing to be set free. If, at this point, parents show their children that they think them capable of great things and of standing on their own two feet, this stage will become a creative, rather than a destructive, phase in the child's life.

Sometimes it is worthwhile to meditate on the Gospels from the perspective of God's anticipating trust. What a mighty advance of trust Jesus gives Peter from the first moment that he calls him. At the Last Supper, when Peter brags, "Though all become deserters because of you, I will never desert you" (Mt 26:33), Jesus answers with a prayer for him and speaks of a great new beginning, "when you have turned again" [that is, repented]. The sad look that Jesus gives Peter after his threefold denial, as well as the triple crowing of the cock prophesied by the Lord, are reasons for John *not* to turn away from Peter after Peter's shameful failure. John doesn't desert Peter, but draws after him by imitating the advance of trust that Jesus had clearly made (see also Jn 20:3–9).

The salvation community of the disciples is supposed to be marked by mutual trust and constant readiness to go on giving fresh advances of trust to one another. With the disciples as models, no room should exist in the Church for such structures of mistrust as systematic spying, anonymous denunciations, or loyalty oaths that make for dishonest conformism.

The fraternal correction that Christian traditions speaks of would be better modeled after the encouragement that should exist among brothers and sisters. Even if called by another name, the whole style and tone of giving an unavoidable correction should be enveloped by an unwavering advance of trust so that the person being corrected can truly see and feel this genuine encouragement.

An advance of trust that flows from a deep reverence for God's grace at work restores to the interlocutor, if necessary, the awareness of his or her own dignity. An unsurpassable example of this restoration is the conversation of Jesus with the Samaritan woman at Jacob's well (Jn 4). He takes this unfairly despised woman and turns her into a messenger of the Good News—an apostle. I think that astonishing miracles of renewal would occur if our Christian life and our communities were thoroughly penetrated by a similar spirit of an advance of trust.

Don't object that such behavior is unrealistic and too much of a risk. My answer is: Just try it! We need to try to continuously shape our thoughts and efforts in a grateful focus on the constant offer of grace, the unceasing advance of trust, on which and through which we live. We need to keep pulling ourselves together again and again. In addition, let us gladly remember the many different times when dear persons unhesitatingly gave us an encouraging advance of trust. Be creative in the ways you cheer up yourself and others through the gift of trust. Be sure not to do it condescendingly, but gratefully, in thankful memory of how often God has wonderfully anticipated your needs.

Trust yourself as well, and believe that you can accomplish great things. Give yourself, as you do your neighbor, the necessary advance of trust, above all when you have failed and failed again. A small dose of moderate mistrust toward yourself and an equal dose, no larger, of mistrust toward others can make you careful, so that you build your trust all the more gratefully and solidly on God's obliging love. You will see: your Garden of Paradise will continue to bloom.

19

The Virtue of Contrition

The virtue of contrition—at first blush not quite a positive one—revolves around a series of concepts that reciprocally complete one another. Christian tradition used to speak a great deal about "continuous conversion" by which was meant a constant readiness to repent. This preparedness for repentance is an awareness of being "on the way," caught in the fruitful tension between our knowledge of what we ought to be doing and, on the other hand, a restless peace with our own imperfections. We acknowledge this tug of war on the one hand, but do not remain stuck there on the other hand. The dynamic tension of the virtue of contrition lies in its call—one that penetrates deeply into the heart—for a radical *yes* when faced with our lofty vocation to follow Christ.

The vice contrary to contrition is that of self-satisfaction—a vice that is bound up in one way or another with spiritual laziness. In the worst case, the absolute opposite of contrition is unrepentance: one refuses to convert or to set out on the way to fulfill, step by step, one's own vocation.

Contrition does not avoid looking at past sins and shortcomings. With a healing pain, it surveys the damage done not only to one's true self, but, above all, to the coming of the Kingdom of God in us and around us. This admission of damage brings on a longing to make reparations insofar as this is possible.

Readiness for constant conversion is characterized by an unwavering gaze at the goal of our noble vocation: "So I do not run aimlessly, nor do I box as though beating the air; but I punish my body and enslave it" (1 Cor 9:26–27).

Paul gives unsurpassed expression to this purposeful orientation: "Not that I have already obtained this [the resurrection from the dead] or have already reached the goal; but I press on to make it my own, because Christ Jesus has made me his own. Beloved, I do not consider that I have made it my own; but one thing I do: forgetting what lies behind and straining forward to what lies ahead, I press on toward the goal for the prize of the heavenly call of God in Christ Jesus" (Phil 3:12–15).

Christian contrition is constant conversion to greater depth and consistency. It also means returning again and again to the painful struggle between the ingrained selfishness of individuals and groups on the one hand and of redeemed love on the other. That redeemed love proves itself in the tireless, liberating solidarity of salvation. As important as the image is of the individual struggle against every form of slavery to sin, that image must nevertheless be completed by a community context.

Constant conversion also implies a process of growth, of

interiorization, ripening, and bearing fruit in justice, stead-fastness, peace, love, and kindness. It also means unflinch-ingly exposing every form of selfishness in one's own heart and in the heart of the community.

Paul comes right out and names those evil offspring of enslaving selfishness that Christians had to struggle against back then: "Fornication, impurity, licentiousness, idolatry, sorcery, enmities, strife, jealousy, anger, quarrels, dissensions, factions, envy, drunkenness, carousing, and things like these" (Gal 5:19–21). This struggle calls for determination. But Paul leaves no doubt in the mind of the Galatians that the unmasking and overcoming of the dark, enslaving powers in us and around us is ultimately and effectively achieved through bearing fruit in holiness and justice: "The fruit of the Spirit is love, joy, peace, patience, kindness, generosity, faithful-ness, gentleness, and self-control" (Gal 5:22–23). Then Paul returns to the image of the spiritual struggle that has now been decided: "And those who belong to Christ Jesus have crucified the flesh with its passions and desires" (Gal 5:24).

Contrition as an expression of the constantly advancing spirit of conversion is not really about special works of penance, such as fasts and mortifications, but about the unflagging struggle against every form of tensed-up selfishness and spiri-tual laziness. Putting it in a more positive way, repentance is concerned with the ongoing process of purification from stub-bornness, self-interest, and group egotism, about growing zeal for the cause of the Kingdom of God. Thus, we gradually overcome every form of paralyzing laziness and superficiality.

20

The Virtues of Patience and Holy Impatience

The virtue of patience covers an uncommonly broad and demanding territory. Patience, especially in suffering, is an irreplaceable part of being a follower of Christ until the last full *yes* in the face of death. Patience is also a sign of full human maturation.

True patience drawn from the power of conformity to the will of God is a healing force of great power. It grants inner peace and gathers our best energies. It is the serene *yes* to any form of suffering that can at once mobilize our efforts and concentrate all our healing forces on true recovery. In certain stages of sickness, the conscientious application of all the directives of the healer and his or her helpers calls for a great expenditure of care and patience. True patience has nothing to do with inert acceptance of sickness or aging. Patience is a gathering together of all the needed forces. It avoids, above all, every form of wasted energy as well as laziness. We especially need the virtue of patience *in dealing with ourselves and with our neighbors.*

In the struggle against our defects and our harmful attitudes, we need a powerful combination of patience and holy impatience. Often we see people engaged in unsuccessful and tension-ridden struggles against their own weaknesses wherein the strugglers fail to give themselves enough patient self-love and healthy self-respect. Once a psychotherapist sent me one of his patients in the hope that perhaps I could do a better job than he in lifting the patient's spirits. After our second conversation, I found myself saying: "May I ask you a question that I find embarrassing? Do you sometimes slap yourself in the face, perhaps in front of a mirror?" The woman was quite astounded and asked in turn: "Whatever made you come up with that question? I've never told anyone about it before. But your guess is true." She added: "When I get really impatient with myself, I sometimes go through this ritual of self-punishment." The solution for this woman lay in stirring up in her grateful admiration for God's patience with us and for his gentle invitation to imitate his patience and realize that despite all our weaknesses he loves and treasures each one of us.

Patience as the accumulated power of self-love and self-discipline directed toward our own character goes hand in hand with the practice of patience toward others. In this context, I would like to return once more to a discussion of the advance of trust. Let us try to admire and imitate the gift of trust that God continuously makes to us as a concrete and healing form of redeemed self-love. This attitude, one that should be continuously deepened, has nothing in common with laziness. It is rather a fruitful dialectic between healthy patience and healthy impatience. It means working assiduously on ourselves without losing strength by giving in to too much impatience.

Patience with oneself and patience with others are twins that should never be separated. Each one has to be understood as a share of the unfathomable patience of God with us all, with me, and with you. Sometimes, it strikes us as really difficult to cope with certain mistaken attitudes of our fellow men and women. In such cases, I see the best way out as taking time to admire the fact that God has so often and for so long had patience with us despite all our mistakes. Here we can only praise God and thank him. And what finally is the best way to express our thanks? There is no mystery here: by imitating the patience of God with us and our neighbor.

I know people who think that from time to time they have to treat themselves to a regular explosion of impatience with themselves or with others. Any person who employs this tactic should just watch as this impatient explosion occurs. He or she will not be able to deny that these episodes of letting off steam only become more frequent and more intense.

A much better solution is to collect oneself for a few moments, breathe deeply, breathe in the love and kindness of God and, in all simplicity, pray to God for patience. In this situation, a self-imposed penance might help a good deal, for example, every time impatience arises and a blowup at others occurs, one should contribute an hour's pay to a hospice or to some other good cause. If necessary, the self-imposed penalty can be made even stiffer. Patience is worth the effort. It really isn't worthwhile to squander our precious energies through untamed impatience.

21

CULTIVATING THE VIRTUE OF HEALTHY DOUBT

Along with the grace and art of wonderment, the virtue of meaningful doubt is an irreplaceable companion on our way to more light and to fuller truth.

In addition to meaningful doubt, other kinds of doubt also exist. There is a frivolous kind of doubt that reveals an abyss of irreverence and possibly also a severe lack of sensitivity. There is another kind of doubt that grows out of mistrust and then awakens and deepens that mistrust.

There is also an excess of doubt that involves the constant and unsettling shifting of perspectives. Instead of focusing above all else on the Beautiful, the Good, and the True that is accessible to us, we needlessly drill away at these with our doubts.

But there is and must be doubt as a virtuous attitude, a thoughtful expression of the prudent search for more light. Meaningful doubt frees us from naiveté, credulousness, and uncritical repetition of other people's ideas.

As parents, educators, teachers, and preachers of the

Good News, we will not presume on our own naked authority. On the contrary, we will prize probing questions, even those that arise from doubt.

We ourselves have to sincerely confess our doubts, even in questions of faith. Often enough doubt is a radically honest attitude in the quest for more light and fuller truth. Simply to repress doubt across the board in conversation and dealings with others, or even in our own hearts, is sick and spreads further sickness. Doubt as a defense mechanism against demanding truth is unhealthy, but doubt in search of truth, completely honest self-questioning, and honest questioning in serious dialogue are all necessary. The route from naive, childish faith to grown-up faith demands careful groping forward, inquiry, and follow-up questions that are an indispensable component of this journey and demonstrate an authentic love for the truth.

Traditional manuals of dogmatic theology and ethics categorize statements on faith and morals to indicate the degree of approximate or complete certainty they contain: truth of faith, common doctrine, reliable thesis, probable opinion, and so on. The new *Catechism of the Catholic Church*, however, drops these distinctions—at a very high price. Now, alongside actual dogmas and clearly revealed truths, the *Catechism* lumps statements that are scarcely tenable, for example, the "doctrine" that, according to God's original intention, humans were physically immortal. In other words, physical death for human beings is supposed to be punishment for Adam's sin. Given the worldwide protest over this claim, it will no doubt be omitted in later editions.

The Christian adult, or the person striving for Christian adulthood, can and sometimes should allow room for doubting whether the latest sermon at Sunday Mass jibes with sound belief. Even Vatican documents in general require no more than a "critical" endorsement or provisional acceptance. We accept them with a certain reservation until we can get "a better understanding," that is, a greater degree of clarity within the community of faith.

In view of our human limitations, the mystery of belief in an infinitely wise God requires a high degree of caution when we talk about faith. Frivolous doubt is a vice, a stumbling block on the road to faith and to recognizing and doing the truth. By contrast, healthy doubt is an attitude of openness, of seeking the light, of ripening into the virtue of criticism, of growing reverence in the face of mystery. Voicing one's doubts, of course, has to be more than just honest; it also has to keep in mind the circumstances of the listeners and readers. Honest doubt, including an appropriate expression of that doubt, calls for something like the art of midwifery or maieutic, as Socrates long ago understood. An honest seeking together on the basis of meaningful doubt engenders and strengthens both the love of truth and the creative quest for it.

22

The Cheerful Virtue of Joy

A cheerful heart and a cheerful disposition are precious gifts for both those who have them and for the world around those who possess these virtues. Holy Scripture often reminds us of the many good reasons for rejoicing. Divine revelation is thoroughly and literally Good News, designed to bring us joy.

We rejoice in God's splendid creation. The whole work of Redemption calls out to us: "Rejoice in the Lord at all times." Once we have internalized this message of superabundant joy, nothing should ever again be able to disturb or destroy our inner peace.

I have made it a rule for myself that whenever sorrow and disappointment trouble me, I explicitly recall that I still have more than a thousand reasons for rejoicing in the Lord. And under no circumstances would I want to be unfaithful to my calling which is to announce the Good News and to awaken and strengthen joy. No one should, on my account, be reminded of the warning by Friedrich Nietzsche, "I would like to see the redeemed looking more redeemed!" If the words of comfort we exchange do not immediately help us to drive away unnecessary sadness, then we should remember that our proclaiming of the Good News will never strike a responsive chord if we go about with sad faces. Our whole being, including our facial expressions, should make known to the world that we trace our roots back to the overflowing bliss of God, who has called us to be cocelebrators of his eternal feast of blessedness and joy.

If that still doesn't help us, then we must examine our consciences quite seriously to figure out where the problem lies. Is it petty attachment to earthly goods so that we hang our heads because of some minor loss? Or perhaps it is our oversized egos that are in the way and that feel offended. If something like this happens to you, then make a bold joke, because the trait of hypersensitivity is laughable. Stand with a swagger in front of the mirror and announce to your opposite reflection: "My majesty is deeply offended!" Look at your sour face and tell him or her: "Well, aren't you gorgeous!" *That* will force you to laugh, and the specter of unwarranted sadness will disappear. If you take great care in reminding yourself again and again of the things that you should thank God for, you will soon find, amazingly, that you cannot finish counting all the reasons. Praise God in your heart; and then you will feel a nourishing current of joy.

A big help in cultivating a deep-down joyfulness comes from singing and making music. The Bible speaks also of dancing and leaping for joy. Cultivating joy is very necessary, but do not think just about yourself. Your neighbors need your cheerful face and sometimes a joyful word from you to get them laughing. Don't shy away from occasionally playing the role of the buffoon. Saints like Philip Neri have shown us wonderful examples of how playful jesting can be of effective service to the Lord.

For a long time "Brother Everglad," Saint Francis of Assisi, was tormented by the sad thought that his brothers would become unfaithful to "Lady Poverty" and were in danger of losing the true spirit. Whereupon Saint Clare delivered an urgent and effective sermon: Preach the Good News, she told him, the way you used to! Let the joy back in your heart! The firm intention of being a bringer of joy to others and a passionate concern for infecting others with holy joy are a highly effective guard against the loss of faithfulness.

Dance, too, is a way of expressing and cultivating joy. I'm no dancer myself, but I often do a little jig to God in my room to express my happy gratitude. And, not last of all, we may and should pray for a glad heart and for the art of making others glad.

In rare cases, we may openly voice to others the things that make our heart heavy. But I have made it a clear principle for myself: complaining does not help. It is exhausting and dangerously contagious. Instead, use your time and imagination to keep calling to mind some of our many reasons to rejoice in spite of everything and to let others see a cheerful face for the Lord.

23

The Virtue of Healthy Humor

I am, indeed, quite serious about counting humor as one of the most precious of virtues. A healthy sense of humor has its own way of chiming in with the Beatitudes. Sometimes humor also demonstrates an astonishing power of healing. Humor often relaxes tensions and contributes a great deal to the acquisition and cultivation of serenity. Even the successful joke that flows naturally into a conversation or sparks a lecture is a mark of humor that distinguishes cordial relationships.

In his rich teaching on virtue, Aristotle calls humor by the Greek word *eutrapelia*, meaning "liveliness" or "ready wit." It is astonishing how earnestly the great thinker recommends this virtue. According to him, it is part of being a fully rounded person and helps cultivate pleasant relations with our fellow men and women. As with Aristotle's entire system of virtues, this virtue is characterized by a "healthy mean" between two extremes, namely grim seriousness and inane foolery.

Thomas Aquinas, who also sets great store by the concept of the healthy mean, takes a broader view than does

Aristotle. Unlike the Greek philosopher, Aquinas is no longer concerned with the conscious virtuousness of a self-assured upper class, but with the warm and overflowing cheerfulness of a redeemed humanity—a cheerfulness that can be found among the little people and the poor, as well as the rich.

In the Christian picture, natural cheerfulness and affability are absolutely essential. These two characteristics must be paired with a delicacy and tact for the feelings of others. The focus is no longer, as it was in the classical Greco-Roman doctrine of virtue, on self-perfection, but on the overflowing of love received as a gift. A healthy sense of humor is a significant mark of this overflowing and redeemed goodness that can cheer up other people.

Humor is a talent that remains authentic provided we understand it as a gift to be passed on. Humor, as we have already stressed, has to do with a spontaneous kindness of heart. Here we can refer to the great thinker and religious founder, Confucius. In his four sacred books, he speaks wonderfully about the four most precious gifts of heaven's way, or Tao. The first of these is kindness of heart which is the fountainhead of politeness, community spirit, and justice. Confucius says emphatically that the gift of politeness is infinitely more than an art learned in front of the mirror or a form of self-satisfaction. Politeness, of which I believe humor is a component, essentially derives from kindness of heart.

In the view of Confucius, where kindness of heart is su-

preme and all virtues are understood, honored, and cultivated as "gifts of heaven," we can also see the outlines of
humility and serenity as powerful ways to establish community.

People gifted with a true sense of humor do not put themselves on a pedestal. They do not look down on others, and
so their humor never injures or humiliates. One feels accepted and encouraged. Humor is something of a random
shot, and it can sometimes make people feel embarrassed.
But it doesn't wound, even when it challenges us to self-
reflection. Humor is always obliging, it fosters a common
search for the Good, the True, and the Beautiful. It is part
of humanity's nobility.

An example may clarify this. Pope John XXIII, a man
with an especially keen sense of humor, was listening once,
in a private audience, to a long litany of self-praise by a
monsignor who very much wanted to be a bishop. Finally
the pope interrupted him and asked innocently: "Could you
now give me the names of the people to whom the credit
goes for these great achievements?" The monsignor promptly
replied: "Unfortunately that is not possible. I had to do it
all by myself." To which the pope said: "O my friend, I can
understand how you feel; because one night my guardian
angel woke me up from a dream and whispered, 'Hey! Don't
take yourself so seriously.'"

To sum up, people gifted with humor are extremely tact-
ful, even when they have to issue a reprimand. They know,
and let the other person know, that we are all in the same

boat. They include themselves as a matter of course. This "matter of course" is a result of kindness of heart. The genuine humor of the redeemed has something relaxing and liberating in it. It establishes and strengthens community and in all things assigns the honor to the Giver of all gifts. How poor our world would be without the virtue of humor which often flashes out precisely when we think the situation is bad enough to make one cry.

24

Irony and Satire As Christian Virtues

In the great Buddhist tradition of pure consciousness and pure serenity, apart from the simply good and the incurably negative, there are a variety of intermediary things that can be transformed into goodness. I would rate irony and satire as two of these traits that can be so transformed, even though they have a biting quality that can easily cause hurt, and they may readily degenerate into a sarcasm that can pull others to pieces.

If I include myself, however, as a target for the irony and satire, then I stand as exposed and as naked as the other. We become members of the same club. To put it another way, the thorn remains, but we join forces to pull it out. And a wound remains, but we go about healing it together.

Are not we all sometimes tempted a bit by delusions of grandeur? Do not we sometimes act as if the world revolved around us? Of course, I see this more clearly and quickly in terms of my neighbor than with myself. If I follow blind impulse, then I will end up telling my neighbor, more or less: "Don't be so stupid!" Language like that causes pain and digs trenches. Even while playing so rough, I myself am being stupid; it never dawns on me that I, too, am an animal in the same zoo.

In the best tradition of Buddhism, the transformation of the ambiguous into the good assumes a deep awareness that we are all in this together and that only together can we save ourselves from the maelstrom. The Buddhist advice to us is to take a closer look at this state of affairs while breathing deeply and totally consciously, all the while seeking a growing detachment. As a Christian, we have, perhaps, even more compelling reasons and motives to play, as humbly as possible, our part in the game of unmasking and setting each other free: we are all sons and daughters of the one God, brothers and sisters of the one Redeemer. Everything depends on our making a radical and thoroughgoing decision for solidarity in salvation and for reciprocal healing.

Doing this blunts the edge of neither irony nor satire. On the contrary, they become still more apt, more on target. But the target itself now becomes healing, not just for the interlocutor but also for myself, in fact for all of us.

Then the tone becomes completely different, and the words, too, are chosen differently. The bitter game becomes a friendly competition: which one of us will be quicker to say good-bye to our delusions of grandeur or some such temptation? I believe that it is worthwhile to concretize the basic Christian virtue of nonviolence into this same perspective.

Once, Brother Joseph Cascales asks me: "What would

you do if you were infallible?" I would, I tell him, stand in front of the mirror and, with a half smile, say to the face looking back at me: "Have you heard? We are *both* infallible." And I'd go on saying it until my mirror image broke out into loud laughter.

25

The Virtue of Enthusiasm

The capacity for enthusiasm, as I understand it, is an ability to make room for enthusiasm in oneself, and then the capacity or talent for infecting others with that enthusiasm.

Enthusiasm is a kind of joy in God that exists as a silent presence in the heart. It shows itself in a cheerful face. It grows deeper in dialogue with other people who are also gripped by faith. Often, it is seen as a long but quietly flowing brook that suddenly bursts into a flood of enthusiasm that sweeps things in its path along with it.

The Gospel of Luke gives us a matchless picture of infectious enthusiasm. The seventy disciples whom Jesus has sent out to proclaim the Good News come back and report enthusiastically about their experiences. Jesus takes their joy to a deeper level by pointing out to them that their names are "written in heaven." Then we witness a peak experience in Jesus' own enthusiasm: "At that same hour Jesus rejoiced in the Holy Spirit and said, 'I thank you, Father, Lord of heaven and earth, because you have hidden these things from the wise and the intelligent and revealed them to infants; yes, Father, for such was your gracious will'" (Lk 10:21). Here enthusiasm is expressly described as a state of being seized by and filled with the Holy Spirit. It is exultation sharing itself, carrying others away. Enthusiasm is answered by even more profoundly based enthusiasm. The uniqueness of Christian enthusiasm derives from following and serving the Gospel; it is "exultation in the Holy Spirit." It is honored and accepted wholly and entirely as an unearned gift. This is the model that I use for imagining the Church and the community of disciples.

By contrast, in spiritual exercises dedicated to his disciple Pope Eugenius III, Saint Bernard (1091–1153) depicts the Church of the time as a travesty: "All day long there is a clattering and crashing of laws, but I do not hear the law that inspires my heart, the law of love, only the laws of the Emperor Justinian." And there follows a rather long list of kill-joys. But then Bernard gives the pope and his coworkers clear advice about how they can open up to the joy of the Gospel and fill the world with enthusiasm.

Today we must especially get rid of the noise pollution of all-too-earthly thinking, quell all ignoble forms of power, and put an end to endless forms of controls. We must aim to achieve perfect stillness, again and again, in and around us. Then the Gospel can speak to us and, through us, to others. We will reap the most splendid fruit when we can share our enthusiasm and "rejoice in the Holy Spirit."

When in our own lives, in our own communities, in our own local churches as well as in the Church worldwide, enthusiasm is lacking or makes only rare appearances, then we have to thoroughly examine ourselves to see what we have been doing wrong. But, ultimately, we must turn in confidence and pray, "Fill me, fill us, with enthusiasm!"

Wherever the Spirit of God blows, wherever people let themselves be filled with the Spirit of God, Pentecost keeps happening all over again. "All of them were filled with the Holy Spirit" (Acts 2:4).

I have the impression—and I suspect that I am right—that the verse from Luke 10:21 about the powerful enthusiasm of the disciples is for Luke a key to the triumphant advance of the Gospel. When we speak of reevangelization, then I think, above all, of the Church's need for many enthusiastic men and women. We have to ask God for a great grace, a storm of grace, to be greeted with hope and longing.

Enthusiasm has its ups and downs, but it is no flash in the pan. It melts hard hearts, liberates cold hearts, and removes many other obstacles.

We have to seriously examine our consciences: What is going on with us, with me, with our Church, that we sense so little—at times nothing at all—of the storm of enthusiasm on Pentecost?

To restore this enthusiasm, certain obstacles must be cleared away in ourselves and in the world as a whole: are these obstacles faintheartedness? excessive idealism? massive systems of control? embittered criticism from above and from below?

To successfully clear the way we need times and places for silence, prayer, meditation, and, above all, a faith in the Holy Spirit capable of moving mountains. "Come, Holy Spirit," we must rejoice and wish fervently.

26

Generosity

Generosity is a sign of gratitude. It speaks of inner freedom. Everything that we are, that we can do, and that we have is precious; it blesses us and liberates us insofar as we can recognize and honor it all as a gift from the love of God.

Many rich and clever people are wretchedly off because they overlook or downright deny the actual interior dimension of life, the dimension of the gift. The rich man who makes Lazarus search for a few paltry crumbs (Lk 16:19–31) is a poor wretch, a poor devil. The rich person who boasts of superfluous possessions slanders God by implying that "so far nobody has ever given *me* anything." God is blasphemed as a "nobody."

If we really sense and honor the brilliance of all our wealth and power in the presence of God, the giver of everything good, then we will not cling to it. We will not misuse these riches and capacities for our own self-aggrandizement and false self-assurance. We are not practicing some sort of idolatry; we are and we will be evermore generous, free to give and to receive.

For generous persons, all their possessions, capabilities, and possibilities become a treasure stored up in heaven, as they serve the needs of others, honor them, and make them happy.

The miser is the archetypal image of a heartless and wretched person. How much joy would the miser give, how much misery could the miser alleviate? But the miser stupidly fails to invest his or her fortune in heaven, in eternity. The joy that the generosity of noble givers pours out upon themselves and the people they give to is one of the most precious and permanent kind of riches.

Generosity means giving out of innermost freedom for God and for one's neighbor. This virtue is liberating for both sides, for the generous and for those who have accepted gifts reverently and freely.

The generosity with which we perform services for others and remedy others' needs is a gauge of our innermost freedom in God. Without generosity, freedom as a virtue does not exist.

The skinflint is the poorest character—talentless, stupid, and unfree. He or she lets himself be mocked by an idol that has nothing to offer. The generous person, by contrast, is inwardly free and in many ways a promoter of a freedom that stands many others in good stead. And what generous people do for or give to others flows back to themselves, as valuable as ever.

The generous person, rich with his or her gifts, strives successfully to become more and more an image of God, who is absolute generosity. Generous people are free to the extent that they seek to honor not themselves, but honor those to whom they give.

The sometimes remarkable generosity of Christian communities that send help when emergencies strike the Third World actually represents a kind of reparation. It makes up a little bit for the manifold injustices on the part of the rich and superrich one-fifth of the world's population that live in the Northern Hemisphere and is tangled in a huge net of unjustice. These reparations masked as generosity should signal an increasingly loud appeal for fundamental reform of the world economy and the relations between the over-privileged and underprivileged countries.

The objection is often made that such aid is no more than a drop of water on a red-hot stone. Yes and no. The spread and increased networking among the many different organizations calling for a better, healthier world through generosity are a hopeful sign. The increasingly well-organized generosity of such groups also serves the true freedom and liberation of the so-called First World of the Northern Hemisphere as well as the incredibly disadvantaged nations of the so-called Third World.

Private, silent, and largely hidden generosity is good and must not die out. But there is still a need for organized collective generosity. Generosity aimed at enabling people to help themselves has an especially noble, emancipating quality.

Volunteer work, which is on the increase in many countries, is a form of generosity well suited to our time. Young men and women give a part of their lives, their skills, and their kindness to those especially in need of it. It is also a creative expression of generosity toward society: these volunteers are building a better future.

27

Frugality

Frugality is the twin sister of generosity. This noble virtue prompts us not just to give out of our superfluity, but to make creative savings so as to be able to give more.

The miser never has enough. The frugal man or woman wonders what, beyond doing without superfluous possessions, he or she can spare or acquire for the needs of others. Frugal people know how to live. They give themselves the gift of contentment and simplicity, and attain as a result an ever-increasing freedom.

Like Augustine, I see the deepest and strongest source of power for the practice of the virtue of frugality in the cry of "Never enough!" Never enough love for God and never enough love for one's neighbor. Both must keep on growing.

As Augustine says in his *Confessions*, "Our hearts are restless till they rest in you." The more potent this holy unrest, the more we will long for the peace of resting in God's love, and the less likely it will be that we will keep on longing for unnecessary things and more worldly success in areas irrelevant to our vocation to love.

With every advance we make in frugality, the broad region open to the growth of love for God and to sharing God's love for us becomes even broader, more attractive, and more deeply satisfying. This satisfaction silences unhealthy turnings toward instinctual restlessness.

The love that comes from God and leads to God is both delightful and demanding. The pleasure of possessions and the power of success will not blind us or distract us so much if a holy restlessness for a still purer, still stronger love lays claim to all our best energies.

If holy restlessness for God and for communal celebration of his love becomes the chief motivating force in our lives, then the insane and restless need for many little things or for more and more property and possessions will fade away of itself.

The moderate use of worldly goods, supported by holy insatiability, that is, the quest for more and better loving, also becomes a source of genuine contentment. It is not the quantity of transitory possessions but the quality of our relationship to them that makes for our happiness.

Frugal persons who invest their energies in the welfare of the community and of those who particularly need our help share intensely in the joy they bring to others. The experience of such collective joy sharpens the vision of frugal persons even more. To their astonishment they keep discovering still more things they can do without, when their renunciation becomes a source of shared joy.

In our culture and at this point in time, frugality is, on

the one hand, an especially difficult virtue, but, on the other hand, more urgently needed than ever before.

The virtue of frugality has gotten more difficult to practice at this time when such a dynamic and rapid progress is occurring in almost all domains of science and technology. This progress threatens to overwhelm us with waves of new products designed to support an image of affluence which many in our society see as necessary and desirable. This image of affluence is only reinforced by the drums of advertisers pounding in our ears.

What will happen in the near future to children who have been exposed from their earliest days to all sorts of nonstop advertising, especially on TV? Not a few parents try to satisfy their children's endless, ad-inspired wishes by constantly buying them new presents.

The economy wants to flourish. It keeps seductively parading before us colorful and appealing new products. And then our neighbors let us know that *they* can afford the latest novelties. Can we?

And yet, at this moment, frugality has actually become a matter of survival. How many sense and know this? Well, it will not be long before we all get a much clearer picture of the impending need for frugality as a matter of self-preservation. The once enormous supplies of nonrenewable resources are being used up with blinding speed. The by-products of our consumption crush the ecosystem; the earth's protective ozone layer has already been seriously eroded. How long will it be before our planet "runs out of breath"?

Though the gap between the Northern and Southern Hemispheres threatens to become ever wider, let us imagine vividly and concretely what would happen to life on earth if the inhabitants of the Southern Hemisphere were to exploit the planet and waste its resources as do the inhabitants of the Northern Hemisphere. Consider for a moment a typical problem: cars. The massive production of automobiles contributes to environmental degradation. The swelling volume of traffic leads to more fatal accidents and maimings. Air pollution is worsening; respiratory diseases are on the rise. Precisely in this critical area we can now see signs that people are coming to their senses and that the virtue of frugality is getting a chance to be heard. People are asking themselves whether they might not after all manage without a car. They carpool and use public transportation whenever possible.

Soon we shall have no other choice but to swing wide the gates of our culture to a systematic frugality. Otherwise we will be utterly at the mercy of the unculture of consumerist society. The reasons just mentioned are important for an ethics and theory of virtue in which awareness of responsibility plays a large role. Still, we have no rational hope for a turnaround unless we grasp the inner value of frugality for the culture of the person. The virtue of frugality deserves to be displayed in all its attractiveness in individual persons and in our communities as a whole.

PART FOUR

28

The Virtue of Just Kindness, or *Epikeia*

Virtue sharpens the eye for what is good here and now. But for an ordered community life, society also needs legal guidelines.

The Old Testament is full of praise for the law that God gave to Israel. Needless to say, such praise is directed, above all, to the universal law of love for God and neighbor. The law of the Sabbath held a place of honor, guaranteeing a day of rest even for dependents and slaves and regularly gathering the community together for worship. Zeal for the law is among the most important virtues of the Old Testament covenant ethic. But excessive zeal for literal and unconditional observance of hundreds of laws sometimes obscures the center and goal of all law, which is love.

The Gospels offer many examples of how Jesus taught people to concentrate on the commandment of love. No individual law should hinder us from loving our neighbor. This point is given drastic expression when Jesus says: "The sabbath was made for humankind, and not humankind for the sabbath" (Mk 2:27). The way Jesus dealt with the Sabbath, according to the New Testament, is a clear demonstration of the virtue of *epikeia*.

The word *epikeia* comes from Greek philosophy. Aristotle takes great pains explaining it: *epikeia* is the rational treatment of laws and regulations so as not to endanger higher values through literal observance. The concept of *epikeia* is usually applied to difficult situations. One should never sacrifice love, the welfare of one's neighbor, to zeal for the law. To do so would result in injustice.

Saint Thomas Aquinas gives loving attention to *epikeia*. It is especially important when the Church is seen from the standpoint of a community of faith and love. *Epikeia* absolutely does not mean a cheap excuse for doing whatever one wants, but is in the grand tradition that exceptions to the law are valid where literal observance would be a disproportionately heavy burden. Basically, *epikeia* is a "better and kinder justice," which must not be put in chains by laws. In complicated situations, even good laws will not achieve their purpose if the sole reliance is on a system of literal obedience.

In the Eastern Orthodox Churches, the term *epikeia* represents a familiar and traditional concept, but there it usually refers to the attitude of spiritual housekeeping, or *oikonomia*. This noble form of spirituality focuses on the "divine Housekeeper," who is deeply concerned about the welfare of every single member of his vast family. Among the best-known features of Orthodox practice in this respect is the way it has dealt, ever since the Patristic period, with divorced persons. Among the Orthodox, as in Catholic tradition, after a Christian marriage has irrevocably failed, the ideal is lifelong continence. But this continence may not be legally required, especially not when it would turn out to be a snare for those concerned and would harm the children.

At the bishops' Synod on the Family in 1980 in Rome, a large majority of the members asked the pope to let the Roman Catholic Church learn from this honorable tradition. Twelve years later, in a pastoral letter arising out of these concerns, three bishops from the Upper Rhine (Saier, Lehman, and Casper) issued a very careful and nuanced document that pointed out steps that could be taken to implement the attitude of *epikeia* or *oikonimia* in ministering to divorced persons. At the moment, the situation in the Catholic Church is marked by a conflict between deep respect for, and serious practice of, the virtue of *epikeia* (or rational justice) on the one hand and a legalistic zeal linked to the desire for clearly defined controls on the other hand.

We need to look constantly and lovingly to what Jesus did and taught on this point. For the sake of a justice based on kindness, he broke a good number of laws that the scribes had absolutized. His idea was to moderate zeal for the law so as to concentrate all energies on the fulfillment of the double command to love God and to love one's neighbor. The law and passion for the law must always and everywhere serve the greater justice based on love.

The virtue of *epikeia* or *oikonomia* expects of Christians a high degree of discernment and a willingness to take re-sponsibility. This high ideal is served by a whole process of education designed to produce a grown-up Christian. Those involved in the sometimes difficult struggle to reach a re-sponsible, conscientious decision may not be left entirely on their own. But that decision, once they have made it, after suitable counseling, must be respected. On this score we can learn from the great tradition of the Orthodox Churches.

Even though the Roman Catholic Church has so far not adopted their practice, we all can and must to a large extent cultivate their spirituality of *oikonomia*. Without this virtue, our Church would be much poorer.

29

The Virtue of Reciprocity

In his famous words John Donne declared that "no man is an island." We find our true self, or our "I," by turning to the "thou" and the "we" of community. I am myself because the Other, God, calls me into existence and therefore to himself.

The child comes to selfhood thanks to the attention that he or she receives from parents and siblings. The child's ego comes to maturity and fulfillment in loving attention to the "thou" of others. Human self-realization takes place in the triad of thou-I-we. Human life is characterized by this interchange, or dialogue, which naturally involves more than just language. Actions proverbially speak louder than words; indeed, simple looks can say meaningful things and bring happiness.

This thou-I-we perspective sheds light on the virtue of reciprocity. We turn our faces to one another. We look at one another lovingly. We serve as one another's eyes and ears. All this means true communication. We learn to know the Good, the True, and the Beautiful in living with and for one another and, above all, in *listening to one another*.

Reciprocal communication is a very noble and demanding virtue. The first question to be answered is: Are we ourselves good listeners? Do we hear not just separate words, but meaningful discourses and messages? Do we perceive the tone of the dialogue and the expression of love as a call for understanding? While attending to the message that others send us, do we overlook the speaker, the messenger? Do we respond to the speaker, to his or her characteristics or intentions? Are we listening to one another? Reciprocal dialogue must become a basic and significant concern to us. The more the person speaking means to us, the more carefully we will listen and pay heed to his or her concerns, to the men or women themselves. All this finds expression one way or another in the look, the tone of voice, and in all our gestures.

If we overwhelm others with a torrent of words, without ever giving them a real hearing, then our capacity for dialogue, for reciprocal exchange, is nil. The best dialogue partners are those who can listen best and then really respond to the speaker and what they have heard.

Action, too, is a message, a substitute or accompaniment for words. And often enough the partner in our dialogue is looking for an answer in the shape of action.

The Christian virtue of reciprocity has its deepest roots and takes on its loftiest nobility from the eternal dialogue of love between the Father and the Word in the Holy Spirit, who is the love that gives and regives itself. Thus, we must not overlook the character of gratuitousness, of loving and

mutual giving. In loving listening and equally loving responses, a reciprocal self-donation takes place. For the word
(in the fullest sense) that I speak is not detached from me.
In it, I turn toward my partner. I express myself, now more,
and now less. In listening to the other, I listen not just to the
sound of the words or to their abstract meaning, but to the
person communicating. And I spontaneously sense it when,
even though it may be unexpressed and not yet capable of
expression, my dialogue partner really means my own self
that turns to face me.

An enlarged capacity for reciprocal dialogue is a decisive
virtue necessary for the good of every community, every
society, and every culture. But this virtue is especially needed
in the Church, whose very life derives from an overflowing
dialogue with God and a response to it. In the relationship
between Church authority and the community of the faithful, capacity for dialogue is the precious elixir of life. Con-
versely, the harsh truth is that those who do not listen, in
the end, do not get listened to.

This capacity for reciprocal dialogue becomes even more
critical when it comes to official, infallibly intended discourse
or doctrines of the highest Church authority. The much-
abused First Vatican Council delivered an extremely clear
statement on this point. The solemn constitution *Pastor
Aeternus*, which defines papal infallibility, makes a sharp
demarcation. It says that the pope can declare a dogma infallible *if* he makes use of all the means made available by
Providence in order to question closely the conviction of

the faithful and their pastors about the issue being considered. Only on that basis can he infallibly declare whether and how a statement corresponds to the revelation of Scripture and Tradition.

At the ordination of priests and the consecration of bishops, I would like to see the candidates' ears anointed and God's grace invoked so that the consecrated individuals may prove to be good listeners who heed the Word of God and with great love attend to what people are telling them.

30

Tolerance

The three great religions that can be traced back to Abraham—Judaism, Christianity, and Islam—have demonstrated, at times, peaceful respect for differing views and, at other times, cruel cases of intolerance. Even during the persecution of the early Christians, persons of exemplary tolerance appeared. One case in point is the Jewish council member Gamaliel who spoke against the persecution of the disciples. Although not a supporter of the disciples, he remarked in Acts 5:38-39: "So in the present case, I tell you, keep away from these men and let them alone; because if this plan or this undertaking is of human origin, it will fail; but if it is of God, you will not be able to overthrow them." With these words he echoed the meaning of Jesus' parable about letting the wheat and the weeds sprout together as found in Matthew 13:24–30.

Christians themselves turned intolerant as the Christian world expanded. Though the Constantinian alliance between Church and state opened with decrees of tolerance, very quickly things turned around. Non-Christians were merely tolerated. Up until the Reformation, the Church maintained a marginal tolerance of Jews and non-Christians, including Muslims, but highly intolerant of "heretics," above all those who had been baptized in the Catholic Church and who secretly practiced their previous faith, for example, the Marranos. The most deplorable expression of this intolerance was the Inquisition and its burning of Jews and heretics in so-called "acts of faith."

After the bloody religious wars between the Christian Churches, the princes of the various denominations began thinking about tolerance. But this wasn't really so much an expression of the virtue of tolerance as an attitude motivated by reasons of state. An ersatz tolerance still denied full civil rights to Christians who were not of the same confession as the prince or ruler. Of course, there were always occasional enlightened individuals who practiced real tolerance out of sincere respect for the consciences of others.

In the Catholic Church, even up until the last century, one heard the saying among conservatives: "Only truth has rights. Error has no rights." As always, the rule is that those who imagine themselves, unlike the others, to be in full possession of the truth will behave more or less intolerantly. A truer tolerance dawned with Vatican II. The Council's statements on freedom of religion, ecumenism, and relations with the non-Christian religions are classic expressions of real tolerance, promulgated with a loving eye for all the goodness and truth that we can learn from other faiths.

Humanity has at its disposal a precious legacy of truths

and insights into values. Above all, it has a heritage of virtues. But no one has a monopoly on the possession of truth, values, and virtues. Instead of monolithic monopoly, our epoch is increasingly characterized by a conscious cultural pluralism. The Church has, at all times, been marked by a great deal of variety, even though this variety is expressed in the one faith and the singular solidarity found in the imitation of Christ. This very variety, however, is not a burden but an enrichment and an unceasing stimulus to learn more and more from and with one another. This variety even manifests itself within the same family: we complete and enrich one another. The prerequisite for this enrichment is precisely the virtue of tolerance, which is more than merely putting up with someone. A paraphrase of this virtue would be: mutual acceptance in mutual respect.

Tolerant people are not blind, and they do not pretend not to notice the less good and downright evil qualities and views of others. We become tolerant to the extent that we are aware of our own limitedness, our own shadow. Tolerance flourishes to the degree that we are thankful to our fellows for accepting us despite our shadows and mistakes.

Truly tolerant persons discover, first of all, the good in others and in themselves. Those who always look first and foremost for the negative do not like either themselves or others. The virtue of tolerance proves itself especially when others contradict us and get on our nerves because of the way they are. Here we should find help in the obvious truth that we cannot be thankful enough for the fact that God lovingly accepts us with all our shadow sides and keeps on giving us a fresh advance of trust.

One touchstone for true tolerance is the treatment of foreigners and refugees who need our respect and help. If tolerance evaporates when it starts making demands on us, then we are still very deficient in this crucial virtue.

In this era, when so many different worlds have come together, the Christian community needs a high degree of reciprocal tolerance, between both individual persons and different groups.

Whenever people try to enforce conformity, there can be no true tolerance. At a time when so much is in transition and many things have to be questioned, pope, bishops, and pastors sorely need the virtue of tolerance as an expression of respect for the conscience of every individual and in the common concern for Christian adulthood.

Tolerance is a much-needed antidote to a culture filled with conflict. If tolerance binds us together, then we can tell one another as politely as possible that we do not agree.

Intolerant people always behave as if they were infallible. They entrench themselves behind "convictions" that in reality are only preconceived opinions. They make themselves incapable of looking into the other side of the argument.

I believe that the virtue of humor is a good counterpoint to every form of acting infallible. A sense of humor can keep whispering to us, "Hey, don't take yourself too seriously!" This relaxed acceptance of oneself and others is a fruitful companion to the virtue of tolerance.

31

Nonviolence

As representatives of the true capabilities of the human race, people like Mahatma Gandhi and Martin Luther King, Jr., constitute a qualitative leap forward as exemplars of a virtue that should be especially dear to all real Christians: the virtue of nonviolence. Gandhi was right to see in nonviolence a central—if not *the* central—all-embracing virtue.

Jesus' message of loving to the utmost unleashes a liberating and healing power and unmasks the diabolical destruction resulting from violence, hatred, and animosity. Jesus, the Servant of God, who is proclaimed in advance by the Servant Songs of Second Isaiah, is the embodiment of solidarity in salvation. He is the light of the nations. He opens blind eyes and leads those who are his out of the fatal slavery of hatred, lust for power, and vindictiveness (Is 42:7). "Surely he has borne our infirmities and carried our diseases" (Is 53:4). "But he was wounded for our transgressions, crushed for our iniquities" (Is 53:5). "'He committed no sin, and no deceit was found in his mouth.' When he was abused, he did not return abuse; when he suffered, he did not threaten" (1 Pet 2:22–23, after Is 53:9). The driving force and ultimate goal of Jesus' nonviolence is *conciliatory love*. He wants to make enemies into friends and to turn us sinners into saints.

Herein lies the unprecedented radicality and loftiness of nonviolence. Unbounded love disdains the degrading recourse to violence. It is stronger than death. It conquers in suffering and even in death. And its victory is the healing, saving transformation of the enemy, the sinner.

This powerful healing predicated on nonviolence is the gift in which Jesus wants us to share. The conversion to nonviolence begins with an amazement that arises in us when we discover that God believes that we are capable of such great, unheard-of things. It is clear to us that *we* cannot trust ourselves to achieve such things on our own. Thus, our astonishment unites with gratitude and petition. "Lord, increase our faith, strengthen us in trust, enkindle in us this love that you brought into the world in Jesus."

We have to keep looking up to Jesus in order to see how he lived nonviolence and reconciling love. When Peter has just denied him three times, he looks him compassionately in the eye, reminds him of his promise to pray for him, and calls him to renewed friendship. In the worst state of humiliation, nailed to the cross, despised and rejected, he cries to the Father, "Forgive them!"

And it is just this liberating nonviolence, this powerful reconciling love that he calls us to achieve and enables us to experience through the power of the Holy Spirit. He sends the Spirit to us, not the least of all on account of his reconciliatory love with which he was ready to face death. This crucial point decides whether our faith is authentic or not. Nonviolence thus becomes the ultimate proof of our trust and our love.

Our world is full of violence. How often do spouses abuse each other? How often do parents disgrace themselves by violence against their own children? Cain's murder of his brother Abel recurs a thousand times over. The proud world powers have in their arsenals enough means of destruction to wipe out the human race and all life on our planet many times over. In what seems like unending ecological crimes, we do so much violence to our planet that, unless we mend our ways, we will choke on the consequences of our own violent depredations.

This situation of violence must be confronted today by anyone preaching the Gospel who ought to demand that we commit ourselves with heart and hand to the virtue of active nonviolence. Mere words no longer suffice here. The appeal is aimed at every individual, at families, nations, but above all at the responsible elites in the world and in the Church.

Those who believe in Jesus' nonviolent reconciliatory love and his mission from the Father will open themselves in prayerful astonishment to this calling, with the firm resolution to give their all so that everyone may understand. There *is* in fact a way out. The royal road of creative nonviolence is the modern-day star of the Magi. Anyone who meditates deeply on Isaiah's four Songs of the nonviolent Servant with whom Jesus himself is identified will clearly recognize that the texts have nothing to do with purely private virtues. Here there is no way to bracket out politics, public life, and the whole economic system. Here we can see more clearly than almost anywhere else that what's at stake in this game is everything.

Since the topic is virtue, or competence, on which the salvation and well-being of everyone depend, we must proclaim this virtue everywhere by word and example; we must acquire and practice it in every possible mode. On all levels, including the global, clear decisions for nonviolence are long overdue, especially since nowadays war and the military machines that wage it are infinitely more lethal than they were in previous centuries. Virtue still has a future on this planet, but only if the urgent obligation to active, creative nonviolence, including the "conversion to nonviolent defense" is known and acknowledged on all levels and in all domains.

32

Humility—More Than a Moth-Eaten Virtue

For the philosopher Friedrich Nietzsche, humility is not a virtue at all. Rather, it represents the chains of slavery. On the other hand, for the convinced Christian, humility in imitation of Jesus Christ, who bent down to us in love, is a powerful and liberating force. In the case of Jesus' liberating love, humility represents more than an isolated burst of courageous submission. Humility implies firmly and high-spiritedly maintaining our courage for truth, thankfulness, and faithful solidarity.

The essential words of our Christian faith, "God is love," also imply in quite a challenging way, "God is humility." God is the love that bends down to us so that he can lift us up. As far back as the Creation, God reveals himself as humility. He makes the world and human beings not out of neediness, but from the overflow of his all-embracing, all-giving love. He is self-donating love—pure and simple. He calls rational creatures into existence, and as conversation partners. It is not as if he would be mute without us. All creation is a freely chosen echo of the eternal primordial event in God, in which the Father expresses himself in the Word whose essence is the same as his, full and complete and infinitely blissful. Creation is the revelatory radiance of the triune love, in which Father and Son make an eternally blessed gift of themselves in the Holy Spirit.

God is present to us human beings in a truly humble love, elevating us to participation in the feast of his triune love. Everything is pure gift; it does not humiliate the recipient, but sweeps him or her up into participation in this same humbly giving love of God.

God reveals himself as humility and as the source of all humility in the body of salvation history. The child in the poor manger, the Incarnate Word of the Father, proclaims to us in soul-stirring love: God is humility. Divine humility lives and acts in the house of the Holy Family in Nazareth. Jesus sees himself and reveals himself as "one of us." His humility lifts us up. It proclaims and gives us the unsurpassable nobility of the sons and daughters of God.

On the tree of the cross, Jesus' divine yet human humility unmasks the slavery of pride, for which the proud are to blame. In uttermost humility Jesus as the Servant of God reveals the salvific power of humble and reconciliatory love. The entire drama of Redemption is the victorious path of high-spirited lowliness that invites and empowers us to imitate Christ. By means of the virtue of humility, the all-holy God grants us the courage to face the unifying and liberating truth—a truth that pride steals from us. The simple look of humble faith lets us plumb the abyss that reminds us how we emerged out of nothing. This pure grace is a calling to life together with the origin of all life and all happiness.

The power of grace and the humility that flows from it gives us a trembling intuition of the fact that in his gracious humility God bridges the abyss of our origin from nothingness. Beyond that, he gracefully frees us from the cave of our "annihilating nothingness," from the heap of rubble and guilt of our sinful failures by which we have acted freely and have squandered our freedom. We owe this act of freeing us entirely to God's humility.

God is the source of our own power and humble courage that allows us to look our shadows and our burden of sin directly in the face, but never in a way that isolates us from praise for the mighty, humble, purifying, and sanctifying action of God.

I do not think that the happiness of heaven will extinguish in us the awareness of having come from nothing and from unending sin. On the contrary, our realization of the incomprehensible humility of God will become an inseparable component of our heavenly happiness and our blissful praise.

We acknowledge but are still amazed at the all-powerful humility of God. This humility is unsurpassably revealed in the way Jesus served until death: "The Son of man came not to be served but to serve, and to give his life a ransom for many" (Mt 20:28).

Finally, those who enslave others sink more deeply into a

slave's existence. Jesus shows himself as the Lord, as almighty love in humble and saving service. Humility in the imitation of Christ is the courage to serve and the liberating courage to live with one another and for one another in love and justice.

33

The Virtue of *Kenosis*: Gain Through Loss

The virtue of *kenosis*, meaning a letting go or a self-emptying, is closely related to the virtue of humility. Jesus is the matchless embodiment of *kenosis*. In his self-emptying and in his taking on the form of a servant—acts that derive from the overflowing fullness of divine love—Jesus models the ultimate fulfillment.

In the New Testament story, *kenosis,* as applied to Jesus Christ, means that our Redeemer, the Incarnate Word of God, wanted to be like all of us little human beings in everything "except for sin."

Kenosis is by no means the same thing as emptiness or "the void." On the contrary, it is a the necessary prerequisite for becoming the "vessel of election," for being powerfully filled with grace and love. *Kenosis* is the primordial image and supporting ground of Christian humility. Like humility, *kenosis* is a breath of grateful love. It is the nurturing soil of thankfulness. It is the high-spirited courage of lowliness—a courage that flows out from fullness and toward fulfillment.

In the lives of human beings, Christian *kenosis* is the existential knowledge of gratuitousness. As the experience of the gratuitousness of our existence as Christians penetrates our minds more deeply, the more this experience empowers us to achieve a letting go or *kenosis*, so that we may be totally protected by God's hand. Our letting go is the imitation, made possible by God's grace, of the self-emptying of Christ, in the clear consciousness of how much this virtue is endangered by pride and by our clinging to a self-centered ego that at bottom becomes our annihilating nothingness.

The virtue of *kenosis* is only apparent emptiness. In reality, it is mightily at work creating space for the wealth of God's gracious action. It defends against our susceptibility to the powers of pride.

Seen in this way, *kenosis* is the rendezvous point with God, who is purely and simply humility for the humble, but in a way utterly different from us. He can give the riches of his grace only to the humble, to those who let themselves go.

God can only resist pride and let the full go away *empty*. *Kenosis* is the pure vessel that absorbs nothing unclean, but in all things gives honor to God.

I think that the experience of *kenosis* will reach its fulfillment in eternal blessedness. Then we will all be utterly grateful recipients; we will be nothing but adoring gratitude. Those who let go of their selfish concerns and self-centered worries here on earth experience fulfillment in God's own fullness. Through the practice of letting go, we draw nearer to Christ. *Kenosis* receives its fullness and beauty and full effectiveness from the gratuitous self-emptying of the In-carnate Word of God.

The virtue of *kenosis* is a piece of Paradise, a return to the Promised Land. Paradise is always lost when and where thankless humans claim for themselves the gifts of God as their private possession. This inevitably leads to hopeless conflict over the arrogated goods, which have long since lost the radiance of grace. Thus everything becomes stolen property fought over not by owners, but by fences.

On the other hand, wherever Christians decisively live out *kenosis*, all of God's gifts shine again in their original splendor and amiably invite everyone to community, to a glad sharing. This sharing makes those who participate in-wardly free and rich, and in such a way that they attend to the needs of others, just as in *kenosis,* the Incarnate Word of God attends to all of us. So, too, does voluntary renuncia-tion lead to participation in God's joy. Insofar as we imitate his *kenosis,* we are allowed to take part in the loving power of God as his sons and daughters. *Kenosis* is the indispens-able gate to the Paradise of the Beatitudes.

Letting go of tense egoism, self-conceit, and the rage of ownership can be momentarily painful and strenuous, but only as long as thankfulness for the grace of *kenosis* does not completely fill our hearts. But where it has firmly grasped our every thought and wish, the grateful person experiences the process of self-emptying as healing, liberating, and limit-lessly enriching.

In Philippians, Paul sings a hymn of praise to his experience with *kenosis*: "Whatever gains I had, these I have come to regard as loss because of Christ....I regard everything as loss because of the surpassing value of knowing Christ Jesus my Lord. For his sake I have suffered the loss of all things, and I regard them as rubbish, in order that I may gain Christ and be found in him....I want to know Christ and the power of his resurrection, and the sharing of his sufferings by becoming like him in his death....Not that I have already obtained this or have already reached the goal; but I press on to make it my own, because Christ Jesus has made me his own" (Phil 3:7–14).

Kenosis sweeps away useless refuse in the house of our soul, to make room for the wealth of God's love and the service for God's Kingdom. The kenotic person, who has been grasped by the *kenosis* of Christ, is no longer alienated, no longer cramped and on edge, but free in Christ and through his Gospel.

Christians who have entrusted themselves to the *kenosis* of Christ will no longer selfishly ask what more they would like to have, but rather what they can give up in the service of their community and their neighbor, what they can give away. Out of the narrow self, from which the Christian has freed himself or herself through letting go, the true self gradually takes shape. In freely giving away and serving and in growing thankfulness Christians will increasingly experience how great the wealth of God's grace and love is. Rather than any sort of loss, letting go turns into a blissful finding of one's own self.

34

Magnanimity

For the Christian who aims to achieve spiritual maturity, there is no way to overlook the virtue of magnanimity—a virtue that has its roots in humility. The "great-souled" person in the Christian sense is humble. But the reverse is also true: the truly humble person, after the image and likeness of Christ, is great-souled.

Arrogant persons who places themselves at the center of things end up conceitedly staring at his or her own navel. Great-souled Christians, by contrast, see everything from God's perspective, in the light of unearned grace: "The Mighty One has done great things for me" (Lk 1:49). So every Christian can rejoice in his or her way. An indispensable part of being a Christian is a grateful awareness of one's incredibly high calling as a son or daughter of God, as a brother or sister of Jesus.

Magnanimous people know that they can expect great things of themselves—though only, of course, on account of God from whom all things come and in whose service in love we achieve the highest honor. This vision of the gift of greatness through God's grace leads us to the core of a specifically Christian moral teaching. In the language of the New Testament, this principle is called *paraklesis,* or consolation—a word that comes from the same root as Paraclete, the characteristic name for the Holy Spirit. This Greek word can also be translated as Advocate, Comforter, or Encourager. These three meanings fuse into one. In a solemn moment, Jesus promises: "And I will ask the Father, and he will give you another Advocate, to be with you forever" (Jn 14:16).

The word *paraklesis* is used repeatedly in the writings of Paul and Luke. While the word *epiklesis* means the calling down of the Holy Spirit to transform the offerings in the Eucharist, *paraklesis* refers to encouragement in the power of the Holy Spirit. *Paraklesis* also represents a kind of transformation: halfhearted persons take heart, pusillanimous persons become magnanimous.

Then, too, *paraklesis* always means praising the God of all consolation, praise and thanks for the power of his grace. The perspective of *paraklesis* decisively excludes every sort of moralizing, every form of moral drum-beating, because joyless moralizing contradicts the God of all consolation. It also contradicts the abundant grace of redemption, God's call to grace—a call that wants trusting friends, not intimidated slaves. Briefly the meaning and purpose of *paraklesis* can be summarized thus: believe you can do great things, because God himself believes you can.

Moralizing stresses prohibition and control. It is always inclined to increase the number of things forbidden and to intensify the punitive sanctions. The paracletic approach to the New Testament puts the accent on the abundance of redemption, on the high calling of the human race. Hence it stresses the goal-commandments, the attractive power of goodness. The power of *paraklesis* is animated by trust in the mighty grace of God. The boundary-commandments, or prohibitions, acquire their meaning from the all-embracing goal of love, not from a delight in the law itself.

The proclamation of the Ten Commandments in the Old Testament has to be understood paracletically. The law gets its meaning and purpose from the grace-filled covenant. All the commandments stand forth in the light and field of force created by God's salvific action. Thus, we read in the prologue to the Ten Commandments: "I am the LORD your God, who brought you out of the land of Egypt, out of the house of slavery" (Dt 5:6). The commandments as a whole serve the God-given freedom to do good and great things and are summed up in the comprehensive commandment to love God and one's neighbor.

Strictly speaking, God's commandment is not to be understood as a harsh "Thou shalt!" The Hebrew language chooses the expression of a future expectation, "You shall love the LORD your God with all your heart" (Dt 6:5). In other words, God may expect of you that, in grateful recollection of his blessings and of his liberating action, you will love him with all your heart and meaningfully observe the individual commandments to protect your God-given freedom. Along these lines, the ten commandments are followed by an epilogue of happy encouragement to cultivate a thankful memory: "Keep these words that I am commanding you today in your heart. Recite them to your children and talk about them when you are at home and when you are away, when you lie down and when you rise" (Dt 6:6–7).

In the New Testament, there is absolutely no way to miss the paracletic tone of the Sermon on the Mount, above all in the Beatitudes. They conclude in the positive encouragement to honor God in prayer and in our whole behavior as Abba, our dear Father. In all his words and actions (not least of those surrounding the Eucharist) Jesus is clearly encouraging us: Believe that you can do great things, because I believe you can, and the Father does too. He is the one who sends from me to you the Comforter, the Holy Spirit.

35

Noble-Mindedness

Noble-mindedness is a distinguished and attractive virtue. It is the answer to Jesus' call: "I do not call you servants any longer, because the servant does not know what the master is doing; but I have called you friends, because I have made known to you everything that I have heard from my Father....You did not choose me but I chose you. And I appointed you to go and bear fruit, fruit that will last....I am giving you these commands so that you may love one another" (Jn 15:15–17).

Ascetical literature often talks about heroic virtues and classes noble-mindedness as one of these virtues of epic stature. However, I strongly prefer the terms "noble-mindedness" and "greatheartedness" to the term "heroic." This virtue does not imply a requirement to "go above and beyond the call of duty," but it does demand basic attitudes that God has a right to expect from us and really does expect from us, in accordance with the superabundance of Redemption. The thankful, happy Christian doesn't ask: "What else do I have to do?" but, rather, "How can I repay the Lord for all the good he has done for me?" Or, still more: "What does it mean for me now to be a friend of God, a disciple of Jesus?"

Noble-mindedness proves itself in its readiness to forgive, but also can be seen throughout the whole fabric of Christian existence. "Then Peter came and said to him, 'Lord, if another member of the church sins against me, how often should I forgive? As many as seven times?' Jesus said to him, 'Not seven times, but I tell you, seventy-seven times'" (Mt 18:21–22).

Greathearted souls are full of amazement that God keeps on healing and forgiving. For them, forgiving their neighbor is something to be taken for granted, an expression of their gratitude for God's forgiveness and healing.

After fifteen years of being happily married, a wife and mother I know found that her husband had been treacherously engaged in an extramarital affair. After three years of living in the same house with her husband's mistress, the latter was stricken by a serious, incurable disease. She had no one to take care of her. Then, quite unexpectedly, without being asked, the wife stepped up and lovingly attended to her rival. She had not a word of reproach or even a hostile look for her unfaithful husband. Just as in the parable of the Prodigal Son, she took him lovingly back. Finally the husband got up the nerve to ask her: "But how can you be so good to me?" Her answer: "Because God is so good to us." That is nobility.

Fortunately, the whole world has a convincing example of greatheartedness right before its eyes—an example that it has in fact gratefully acknowledged. This example is

Mother Teresa of Calcutta and the good members of her order. They take care of dying people who have been abandoned by everyone else, not out of condescension or to win admiration. Rather, they feel honored that they have been allowed to honor Jesus in these poorest of the poor. Their action is a spontaneous overflowing of praise for what Jesus does for us, for them.

The literature of asceticism speaks of "works of supererogation." Unfortunately this expression may be faulty in two ways: first, it focuses on works, instead of on a permanent attitude; and, second, it creates the impression that the persons involved are paragons of virtue.

I have long been acquainted with a woman doctor working as a missionary. Once, in Ghana, when I was giving courses near a hospital that she had built with money begged from here and there, I tried to pay her an early morning visit. But when I saw the long line of patients, I turned back. At two o'clock that afternoon I tried again, but the line was just as long. That is how it is for medical missionaries, year in and year out. If no one can be found to replace them, they do without vacations with an astonishing casualness. The doctor I mentioned is now in her old age and is a pastoral caregiver for imprisoned refugees. She takes care of them in every way, not in some superior fashion but with reverence and love. That is noble-mindedness and the sort of nobility that keeps humanity together. If we Christians would cultivate this virtue, what a different shape the Church and the world would take.

36

SERENITY

S erenity is a core concept and a leading idea of the great Dominican mystics Meister Eckhart (1260–1327?), Johannes Tauler (1300–1361), and, most especially, Heinrich Suso (1295?–1365). It is an expression of the grateful sense of security one feels in God, an all-embracing basic attitude experienced as the fruit of God's grace at work in us. It is a foretaste of our definitive home-coming to God.

Serenity gives or guarantees a proper perspective. In the face of the splendor and kindness of God, all sufferings and difficulties cease to threaten us. The mystic who has shared in the grace of serenity says confidently with his or her whole heart: "I can still praise God," regardless of the disappointment and pain being momentarily experienced.

Heinrich Suso describes his prayers and struggles for serenity in gripping fashion. On this subject, scholars of mysticism often cite Suso's "tower experience." One time, some despicable colleagues of his wanted to test whether Suso really was as calm and composed as he seemed. They paid a woman to accuse Prior Suso to his provincial superior of having committed adultery with her. The superior believed the accuser, deposed Suso as prior, made him wear a monastic cowl, ordered him to be whipped, and had him locked up in a wretched dungeon. One day, looking down from a tiny window in his prison, Suso saw a little dog playing with a rag. The dog tossed the rag in the air and then caught it again and went on tearing at it, while joyfully hopping about. Suddenly, Heinrich felt his heart grow warm: "If you are the one, Lord, who is playing with me as that dog plays with the rag, then just keep on playing!" From that point on, he was engulfed by a sense of serenity that never left him.

Saint Alphonsus Liguori cites this moving episode in his book *Conformity With the Will of God* and sees in it the perfect illustration of his title. For Liguori, as for Suso, serenity means locating and securing all the powers of the soul in God's saving plan. It is boundless trust and commitment: "May your saving plan be fulfilled in me!"

Those who believe that God is love know in the depths of their heart what they are praying for when they say, "Thy will be done." Serene persons have entrusted themselves once and for all to God's loving will, to his adorable saving will. But since they still know that such serenity is a grace, they do not stop praying for serenity and perseverance.

Serene people have understood what faith means: they anchor themselves in God's salvific will where they know they are perfectly secure. They have a sense, implanted in them by the Spirit, for the right proportions and dimensions. Italian has a felicitous term, "*ridimensionare*," meaning to bring something back to its proper proportions. In believing trust, serene persons look upon suffering and unpleasantness in the light of faith in the Resurrection and providence. They are so penetrated by the spirit of gratitude and praise that nothing can rob them of their tranquil serenity or inner peace. This inner peace was a key notion and part of the message of John XXIII. Security in God and serenity, even in hard times and critical moments, are at the precious core of the messianic experience of *shalom*. It is the deepest peace of the soul that inevitably radiates around all who possess it.

Serenity has nothing to do with a retreat to pure inwardliness or with pathetic self-satisfaction. It is rather a continuous fountain of strength for grown-up Christians—a form of strength that matures them into believable messengers and instruments of peace and reconciliation.

The models of cheerful serenity, such as Heinrich Suso, Teresa of Ávila, Catherine of Siena, and, not least of all, Francis of Assisi, were at the same time humble and frank reconcilers. Precisely because of their innermost serenity and security in God's plan of salvation, they were able to stir up consciences and spur the weary on the path of peace, to create reconciliation and serve all-encompassing justice.

The one matchless and always attractive archetype of serenity is Jesus himself—even, and especially, amid contradiction and suffering. He makes it evident to us that his strength and serenity flow directly from his secure anchoring in the will of the Father. The peak of serenity is his prayer on the Cross: "Abba, Father, into thy hands I commit my spirit, and "Abba, Father, forgive them."

With unique clarity, Jesus recognizes the loving will of the Father and therefore his own vocation as the humble and serene nonviolent Servant of God, who shows himself to be the beloved Son through his long-suffering, healing, and reconciling love.

Let us apply this overview of serenity to the current situation in our Church. In one situation, many women and men feel deeply hurt by the teaching—now explicitly declared by the Vatican to be irrevocable—that according to God's own decision women are absolutely unsuitable for, and incapable of, a full pastoral vocation. In another situation, a great many priests and large numbers of the laity were and are alarmed and shaken by the total ban on communion for divorced and remarried Catholics (unless they promise to completely forego their marital rights with their new spouse). All of us, and not just women with pastoral vocations or the divorced, are affected by these rulings. Many others, as well, suffer, for those who are most immediately involved. And I myself feel deep sympathy for all the bishops, priests, and laypeople who *do not* feel any sadness over this state of affairs.

A woman theologian recently asked me in great pain: "Am I really not allowed to do anything more than get angry over this?" Are we now supposed to lose all heart, become desperate or enraged? By no means: "We can still praise the Lord," holding on even more tightly to God's plan of salvation and looking for ways, through healing nonviolence, to peacefully solve these and other problems.

Needless to say, now is not the time to confuse serenity with weary resignation. Now we have to "heap burning coals" on the hardheaded moralists (see Rom 12:20). That doesn't mean that we may wound anyone. The text from Romans refers to the custom in the ancient world of carefully collecting all the burning coals in a "heap" at evening time, so that the fire in the hearth would not go out. Back then, it was difficult to rekindle the fire. In serenity and creative nonviolence, let us take pains together so that the warm flame, the precious fire, does not go out. Indeed, serenity will help us to prevent that.

37

The Virtue of Frankness, or Parrhesia

For us, the highest and most unsurpassable embodiment of frankness, or *parrhesia,* is Christ. Lovable and infinitely patient, he speaks kindly and straightforwardly to the small and the weak. With incredible patience, he seeks to win the faith of his people, particularly its leaders. On the other hand, with blunt frankness, Christ challenges the proud and incorrigible exploiters of all kinds. With the highest freedom, he has the courage to step forward to uphold the liberating truth even when this action brings persecution and death.

He, who is the truth personified, has every right on his side when he boldly and freely expresses the truth. And, the proof of his frankness is love, for the truth in question here is always the truth of life.

Human beings will gradually come to the truth, to their own truth and, finally, to the truth of God, if they lovingly and patiently seek, think, speak, and do the truth. The issue here, the one that concerns me, is purely and simply the truth of salvation. In order to arrive at this truth, we must be free. And, in it, we also find our true freedom.

Threatened as we are by darkness and sin, we humans have to see ourselves, above all, as truth-seekers. And this true picture of self is possible only in solidarity with all seekers after truth. If, in true union with others, we have found Christ, who is the Way, the Truth, and the Life, then we will never cease to strive to communicate to others this infinitely precious treasure. We do that by bearing witness, in season and out of season, to the highest truth of all.

The foregoing is a framework and living space for the virtue of frankness. We know that we have been recognized and enriched by Jesus, for the salvation of our fellow men and women. It is clear to us that the Christian virtue of frankness can never exist apart from remaining in the truth and doing the truth.

The virtue of frankness never raises the issue of whether our actions and words about the truth of salvation help or hurt us. The crucial point is always whether and how they promote the salvation of everyone. In view of the frankness of Christ, no price for *parrhesia* should strike us as too high.

In the case of Mahatma Gandhi, the virtue of *parrhesia* takes on the form of *satyagraha*. *Satyagrahis* (persons entirely dedicated to, and grasped by, the truth of salvation) know that they do not possess the whole truth. But they will always summon the courage to speak out honestly about what, to the best of their knowledge and conscience, serves the kingdom of truth, peace, and justice.

True *satyagrahis* never break away from the community of truth-seekers. They have a sharp ear and a loving eye for the contributions to truth made by others, including their opponents. Opposition becomes radically detoxified because the so-called "opponent" can sense that his or her share of the truth is getting placed on the scales as well. It is being taken in and made fruitful, as soon as the opponent accepts an advance of trust to join the community's quest for more light. According to Gandhi, the bridge that links us, even with our opponents, is *ahimsa,* loving empathy with our interlocutor, even when he or she contradicts us or turns aggressive. *Satyagrahis* help their conversation partners to greater inner and outer freedom, and thus to more authentic frankness through this perceptible solidarity in searching for and doing the truth.

The frankness of the *satyagrahi* in no way humiliates or degrades the interlocutor. The advance of trust that he or she senses gives additional courage to search even more freely for fuller truth through word and action.

Frankness remains a true virtue. The crucial condition is that frank persons must never let themselves become embittered; they must keep trying to synthesize the humble and community-based search for truth with frank expression of their own convictions and concerns in word and deed.

Truly frank persons are not obsessive "truth fanatics." They love God, the original source of all truth, and they find speaking and doing the truth an indispensable necessity. Because of this, they love and honor with a maximum of empathy every one of their conversation partners and fellow wayfarers, even when they sometimes seem to behave like enemies. This conviction is possible because the frank person understands that the truth born of love and aiming to serve love will ultimately triumph.

38

The Virtue of Grown-Up Obedience

If we have truly made the long-overdue shift from a one-sided ethic of obedience to one based on an ethic of responsibility, blind obedience to other human beings can no longer be given pride of place in any scheme of the virtues. The gifts of discernment and frankness take priority over obedience to humans, including the bearers of religious authority.

Many sinful forms of obedience exist and many horrible demands have been made in its name. The admonition from Acts of the Apostles 4:19 is more pertinent than ever: we must obey God rather than other humans. However, in these times, as ever more people take a rather critical stance toward authority, an astonishing number, with a numbing lack of awareness, continue to follow the dictates of the media, especially of advertising.

By calling for a rather uncritical obedience and by themselves submitting to often immoral worldly authorities, all the Christian Churches share the guilt for the fact that so incredibly many Christians took part in the horrors committed by Stalin, Hitler, and other criminals. If all Churches had trained baptized persons to practice a grown-up—that is, a critical—obedience and a true spirit of responsibility, many wars would never even have started. Above all, Christians would not have cooperated, either actively or passively, with the greatest of horrors—the Holocaust.

The basic school of grown-up obedience is the family. The genuine obedience of husband and wife to each other is characterized by mutual listening and a common search for the best solutions in each particular case. This genuine obedience is greatly endangered by a belief in the subordination and obedience of wives to their husbands on practically every matter.

It is no accident that all children normally go through a period of asking questions. Parents and educators should respond to them seriously, lovingly, and—insofar as the age of their charges allows—thoroughly. In the process, they themselves have to go on learning. Parents must cooperate creatively so that the virtue of criticism may grow out of the questioning phase of puberty. Inopportune and outmoded demands for obedience, especially uncritical obedience, lead either to rebellion or obsequiousness.

Religious obedience has quite an exceptional dignity. In its absolute form, we owe religious obedience to God alone. But just as God's revelation comes to us only when mediated, so, too, the truths of faith reach us only when mediated. The meaning of faith and the authenticity of religious obedience confront a crisis when religious authorities or educators demand all too much submission to an obscure package of doctrines. Education for religious obedience is, above all, reverent. It leads the way to the unfathomable mystery of God and to the living knowledge of Jesus and his teaching. Some leeway must be allowed seekers and doubters; they have to be guided to the gift of discernment—a discernment that must also be focused on the life and teaching of the Church.

All authorities should be tested to see how competent and credible they are. The Church, too, has to allow room on all levels, for questions and complaints, so as to promote the development of adult criticism as well as adult obedience.

Situations where we cannot obey should be acknowledged as painful; and those situations where obedience is obviously called for should be greeted with joy. In modern society, and particularly in modern political life, laws and regulations threaten to proliferate into infinity. As far as we can, we have to rein in this proliferation. In addition, we have to learn to distinguish where obedience is a genuine and necessary expression of communal responsibility and justice and where it would be out of place.

Adult obedience in a democratic state and a democratic society must always go hand in hand with our efforts for a just social order and just laws. We must resist every tendency toward dictatorship and authoritarian behavior that has no concern for the common good and the development of the individual. As far as human beings are concerned, the last word is never obedience but loving, shared responsibility.

Since the goal is grown-up obedience, the most important aspect of the virtue of obedience is our personal and group effort to attain moral adulthood and maturity.

39

Truthfulness

The moral theologian Johann Michael Sailer (1751–1832) has written in great detail and depth about the virtue of truthfulness. In his writings, he stresses complete inner truthfulness before God and oneself. This virtue proves its worth in three dimensions: thought, word, and deed.

Being true in thought is the foundation of the virtue of truthfulness. In our drive for knowledge and truth, are we first and foremost concerned with knowing God and his revelation? In a word, are we concerned first with the truth of salvation? The most brilliant scientist, the most outstanding technician, the smoothest politician, can all be extremely underdeveloped as human beings if they do not care above all and before all else for the true knowledge of salvation. I can still vividly remember a long flight I once took, seated next to a Japanese politician. We wound up talking about (among other things) religion—a topic in which he seemed quite interested. But at a certain point he said: "I really cannot get involved with questions of religion until I have achieved my goals as a politician." Was he not sincerely voicing the attitude of countless other people: salvation, second; earthly success, first?

Thinking truthfully has a great deal to do with our memory and our imagination. Is our memory, together with all our thoughts and aspirations, like a holy temple, where high and noble truths and values hold the place of honor in a meaningful order? Does our admiration and amazement over God's action constantly pour out there like incense? In the final analysis, many people would have to admit that their memory is a sort of garbage dump, with everything thrown in this way and that. A memory stamped by gratitude, admiration, and appreciation of the highest values and truths leaves no room for unreasonable bitterness or ignoble thoughts and ideas.

People who want to be true in their thoughts do not get lost in pettiness and finicky behavior. They have no time for useless speculation. Being truthful in one's thoughts means openness to divine revelation, to everything that is part of the kingdom of love, the Good, the True, and the Beautiful. Those who are completely true in their thinking hear the swelling, blessed echo of the Good News, the unfathomable truth of faith, in the depth of their hearts.

Being truthful in our thoughts and aspirations promotes the joy of discovery. Ever new domains of the True, the Good, and the Beautiful open up. Increasingly, too, one sees everywhere, but especially in our neighbor, the Good and the Beautiful. This seeing of God in our neighbor is an indispensable prerequisite for sound and healthy human relationships. As the Good becomes visible in our neighbor, we see more and more opportunities to encourage and honor others and to turn them into friends and companions for peace and justice.

Being truthful in thought spontaneously gives rise to *being true in speech,* in all the manifold realms and forms of communication. In today's world, the task of cultivating truth in speech and the other media goes far beyond the familiar personal domain. We are all called upon to make our contribution, so that all the many "stations" sending messages in the modern world may broadcast what is true and meaningful. We are partakers in many decisions in the area of communications, for example, through our choice of newspapers and magazines, and not in the least, through our choice of what TV programs and movie videos to watch.

We all have thousands of old and new opportunities of "passing on" the truths of our faith, of attesting to them and proclaiming them in an attractive form. Do we fully realize how much the many-faceted contemporary media are entrusted to everyone's shared responsibility, but especially to those who are highly gifted in this area? Are we more or less passive, surrendering ourselves and others to whatever noises happen to be loudest at the moment? Or do we do what we can to achieve the necessary competence enabling us to make a positive contribution in this crucial sector of modern life?

The peak of truthfulness in the broadest sense is *doing the truth in love,* because ultimately there is no separating truth and truthful love. At the highpoint of the Sermon on the Mount, Jesus speaks with unmistakable decisiveness about doing the truth: "Everyone then who hears these words of mine and acts on them will be like a wise man who built his house on rock" (Mt 7:24). Translating the Beatitudes and all the directives and truths of the Gospel into action strengthens and deepens our relationship to the truth of salvation.

The three dimensions of truthfulness (in thought, word, and deed) are comparable to the intradivine *perichoresis,* or *circuminsession*—the fruitful, dynamic interexistence of the three divine Persons. Those who in the hour of decision resolutely turn the truth of love into actions find for that very reason ever new horizons open up in thinking, communicating, and doing the truth. The three dimensions of the truth are as inseparably similar and analogous as are the three divine Persons. The high point of truthfulness, then, is the joyful, loyal, and creative doing of the truth—the doing of which is a promise and a pointing to the eternal feast of the truth and truthfulness of love.

40

Sincerity:
A Sign of Upright Behavior

Deep sincerity in everything we say and do in our lives is a lofty personal value. It is also a vital good for the whole community.

Every church community and the Church as a whole should be a privileged space for absolute sincerity and transparency in all relationships. Herein is a key problem for today's Church, in which a powerful trend seems to exist toward increasing centralism, an obsession with maintaining control and enforcing conformism. There is also a propensity to absolutize authority and visible obedience down to the tiniest detail. All this is at war with the call for upright behavior, complete transparency, credibility, and radical sincerity.

In German, the word for *sincerity* is *Ehrlichkeit*. This word is related to the word for "honor," *Ehre*. Honor and reciprocal honoring are high social goods and have a great deal to do with human and Christian virtues. Whom do we honor with our sincerity? We honor our companions on life's way, our conversation partners, our community and, of course, our Church as well.

We are all hit hard by a loss of sincerity. Damages and losses in this area cast a shadow over and diminish our vocation to honor God individually and communally. God honors us by creating us as persons in community, not as mere servants assigned to perform certain tasks. He offers and gives inconceivable honor to all those who gratefully accept the calling to be sons and daughters of God. We honor him and, therefore, are honored by him to the extent that we mutually honor one another as brothers and sisters before God. So the first demand is that we be sincere, upright, and honorable to one another. If we are, then we earn respect in the eyes of non-Catholics and non-Christians. Sincerity within the whole body of the Church is now more than ever an indispensable prerequisite for our testimony of faith before the world.

Our honor before God has its roots and its dimension in our gratitude and fidelity before him. It is not measured according to the external honor that we receive from men and women, if that is out of line with our inner honor. As long as we are primarily concerned with what people think and say about us, or how they show us signs of honor, our honor with God is not in good shape, nor are we capable of honoring God worthily. Our honor and our sincerity have to be continuous and steady before God and in our innermost conscience. Those in authority who deliberately surround themselves with yeasayers are sinning against their own honor and increasingly turn into the enemies of honesty.

To be sincere, in the fullest sense, means that we may not try to fool ourselves or anyone else by claiming something that does not fully correspond to the truth. Christians who wish to testify to their faith and pass it on, have to be sincere, to be a transparent window. It has become clear to many people that without openness, no real renewal can take place. This requirement applies to the whole of society, but in a very special way to the Church.

It goes without saying that sincerity forbids not just lies, but every form of deception (including self-deception) and whatever contradicts honesty and upright behavior. We have to be honest and sincere with everyone, including our opponents. An unremitting love, and a reasonable advance of trust should characterize our dealings with all people. Yet we should never throw our pearls before swine (Mt 7:6). If we have reason to fear that others will misuse certain information we give them to harm a third party, then we have to keep silent. If necessary, we should even speak evasively.

Still, even in such painful moments, we have to honestly examine what we do or don't do before God and in the light of our own conscience. In confused situations, only a carefully cultivated pure intention can protect us from lapsing into some form or other of dishonesty.

Even when dealing with opponents and people who have at least partially betrayed their own honor, the Christian virtue of sincerity must be maintained. And sincerity is maintained, above all, by keeping our eyes focused on God, who has loved us in spite of everything and who ceaselessly invites us to renew our love for him. He continually anticipates our needs; and thus we should try to do the same thing in our relations with our neighbor.

41

Openness

Openness is a precious talent and virtue. It contains and implies transparency. It has many significant dimensions: openness to the future, readiness to learn and to be transformed. It keeps seeing new perspectives on life, new concerns, and new opportunities. Not least of all, openness means a *heart* open to others. Openness is the radiance of inner truthfulness.

People with this gift are like the proverbial open book in which we keep making new discoveries. But they are also a book which more and more new entries—discoveries, experiences, and insights—are being made.

Openness is, above all, a fundamental attitude toward God, his truth, and his grace. Open people continuously let themselves be showered with both gifts and challenges by the first source of truth and love. Openness makes us inventive and creative. Openness often shows us new horizons and beautiful new vistas in the realm of the Good and the True. Those gifted with openness let themselves be surprised, and, in turn, provide others with refreshing surprises, new insights and opportunities.

Openness is an inestimable endowment that readies us for dialogue. Those gifted with the virtue of openness have many "antennas," which often pick up unexpected new insights and perspectives. My revered teacher, Romano Guardini, was rightly famous as a man with these sorts of feelers. He taught and wrote with an open heart, full of sympathy for his contemporaries and dialogue partners.

When openness is coupled with alertness to the here and now and the gift of discernment, this union creates fruitful simultaneity, contemporaneousness, and a community marching together toward the future. Open people discover and appreciate the opportunities of each moment. This was a great concern of the apostle to the Gentiles: "You know what time it is, how it is now the moment for you to wake from sleep. For salvation is nearer to us now than when we became believers; the night is far gone, the day is near" (Rom 13:11–12). Paul admonishes his readers to openness and at the same time to preparedness: "Be careful then how you live, not as unwise people but as wise, making the most of the time, because the days are evil. So do not be foolish, but understand what the will of the Lord is" (Eph 5:15–17). In context, this means that for those who out of reticence or sleepiness fail to make the most of every moment, of the current time of salvation, for these and only these people, "the days are evil."

Openness flourishes in the fruitful soil of gratitude toward God and toward our fellow human beings. Gratitude is, as it were, the open channel for the reception of new graces, new insights, and new possibilities. At the same time, openness is the fruit of a pure heart, which at all times and in all things is tuned to the wavelength of God's salvific will. We request and cultivate this openness through the prayer "Thy will be done."

Openness is also inseparable from the spirit of community. The virtue of openness is *not* a petty concern for one's own self, but a caring for the common good. This cause is advanced by a constant readiness to listen to one another, to prize the insights and the creative activity of others.

Both openness and readiness prove themselves when faced with the "poor," that is, whoever here and now needs my open eyes and my responsive heart. Those who close themselves off to the claims of others, to their material help and their love have not simply wasted an opportunity, they have caused themselves an enormous loss in openness.

In this virtue, too, I see a kind of "circuminsession": from the virtue of openness flows a fruitful stream of the virtues of purity of heart, sensitivity, wakefulness, and readiness to learn, along with the charism of teaching. In summary, we can offer the warning: Those who waste their time whining and wailing about the evil times and bad people are blocking the channel of gratitude. They become unreceptive to grace and to the call of the moment; they forfeit the most precious opportunities in the here and now. To the praising and wakeful Christian community, surprising new horizons are continuously opening up in the grace offered by each moment, depending upon the degree of openness showed by its members.

42

The Virtue of Chastity

The virtue of chastity deals with the whole domain of the sexual gift of man and woman and with all interpersonal relations insofar as they are marked by sexuality.

I deliberately say "sexual gift," to stress that the sexual dimension of our human existence is a precious gift of the Creator. If this believing perspective is lost, then we have already missed the most essential feature of the virtue of chastity. God's judgment applies to sexuality too: "God saw everything that he had made, and indeed, it was very good" (Gen 1:31). "Then the LORD God said, 'It is not good that the man should be alone; I will make him a helper as his partner'" (Gen 2:18).

No personal "I" is thinkable without the "thou" of the other. We all have our origins in the most intimate I-thou-we of our parents. Our ego-consciousness unfolds in the face of the "thou" of the mother and the "thou" of the father. They meet us as "we" and by each saying "thou" to us they welcome us into this unfathomably rich "we." At our birth, a holy curiosity made them ask, is it a boy or girl?

Either way, they could greet the news as a gift of God. But in this existence that has been given to me now, I am, in fact, a man. I also honor this status as a gift, not the least of all by regarding my sisters, that is, all women, as gifts of God. Very early on, children learn existentially that being a man and being a woman, the connectedness of father and mother, of being a father and being a mother, represents a summit of our "gifted" existence.

This is the foundation on which the virtue of chastity is built: I honor my masculinity, women honor their femininity, in such a way that this works out as a gift for me and you, for ourselves and others. In all areas and in all human relations, we have to see to it that we remain for one another a precious gift of God and become evermore so. If we do this, we have already laid the best and most solid foundation for the virtue of chastity.

The feeling of pleasure is an inseparable feature of sexuality. It would be wrong to look upon pleasure as intrinsically suspicious or even evil. Of course, pleasure must not be made an autonomous value. It must remain integrated into our joy in God, in his work, and especially in our vocation to love. Wherever we cultivate the capacity for love and reverence both for one another and ourselves, we are building the foundation for the virtue of chastity.

One of the preliminary stages of chastity is modesty. It flows organically from the perspective of gratitude for our masculinity or femininity; and it expresses itself in mutual reverence and shared responsibility.

The sensations of pleasure that boys and girls begin to experience at the onset of puberty must not be treated with suspicion, as if they were evil. But it also makes no sense to concentrate too obsessively on them; because we have a thousand other reasons for pleasure and joy. We must not lose our sense of proportion, but foster and cultivate it.

It is false and dangerous to argue that in the area of chastity every voluntary slip-up is by its very nature a serious sin. For example, exaggerated emphasis on so-called "self-abuse" often serves only to make it more of a problem.

Full sexual union belongs in the realm of marriage. It should be celebrated as a highpoint of mutual love. But there is an essential difference between the arbitrary indulgence in sexual relations outside of marriage and the loving union of an engaged couple, especially when external circumstances force them to put off the wedding for long time.

The key to chastity in every way of life is always the cultivation of reverent mutual love, rational self-control and integrating the sexual expression of oneness into the totality of reciprocal love.

Just as the full capacity to love requires faithful, patient practice, so does chastity. The best protection for chastity and the source of its innermost strength lies in the art of bringing joy to others—in all things and not least in matters of human sexuality—and of rejoicing with them in the presence of God.

43

The Virtue of Childlikeness

Thérèse of Lisieux saw the way of childhood as her vocation and her plan of life. As for the meaning of this childlikeness, she made the New Testament her guide.

Childlikeness means, above all, a radical rethinking of our vocation by those of us who are so much a product of society's "performance principle." Jesus presents a child to his disciples and says, "Unless you change and become like children, you will never enter the kingdom of heaven" (Mt 18:2). In this context, the main point is humility before God as expressed in mutual reverence and esteem. "Whoever becomes humble like this child is the greatest in the kingdom of heaven" (Mt 18:4). Mary's *Magnificat* provides the clearest commentary on this idea: "For he [God] has looked with favor on the lowliness of his servant" (Lk 1:48); and "He has...lifted up the lowly" (Lk 1:52).

Jesus identifies himself with children: "Whoever welcomes one such child in my name welcomes me" (Mt 18:5). By his own example, Jesus teaches us to express ourselves like children before God and to have full confidence in calling him "Abba," Father. We experience our childlike condition when the Abba-prayer becomes part of our life plan, our basic attitude: we simply hand ourselves over to God's fatherly love and care. We feel safe and secure. Still, the Abba-prayer also demands brotherly and sisterly behavior. We love and honor God as our Abba, when our love for him proves itself in reciprocal love.

Saint Alphonsus Liguori described the spirit of childhood when he said, "There is no better way to honor God than through complete trust in him." This basic and primary trust gives rise to the experience of security, even amid storms. This form of trust becomes especially clear when we hear Jesus praying from the depths of his heart, "Abba!" on the Mount of Olives and on the cross.

Being a child in the presence of God is marked by a loving knowledge, as the author of the First Letter to John says, "I write to you, children, because you know the Father" (1 Jn 2:14).

In the Letter to the Hebrews, Jesus is quoted as saying, "Here am I and the children whom God has given me" (Heb 2:13). If this truth is etched into our hearts, nothing can frighten us.

In uncomplicated union with Jesus we pray "Abba! Father!" and in uncomplicated affection we love one another with the love of Jesus. Jesus himself takes us by the hand as his beloved brothers and sisters and leads us to the Father. The risen Christ encourages his intimidated disciples by tenderly addressing them as children. "Jesus said to them,

'Children, you have no fish, have you?'" (Jn 21:5). Then Jesus himself prepares a family meal for them.

In summary, let me try to give an image of our calling to spiritual childhood: We entrust ourselves completely to the Abba-Breath of Jesus. We let ourselves be taken up into his love for the Father and for human beings. Thus, we feel ourselves, with Jesus, completely secure in the love of the Father. And in Jesus' Abba-Breath, we learn true brotherliness and sisterliness. Like Thérèse of the Child Jesus, I could not even imagine the coming heaven without this total togetherness as brothers and sisters in the sight of God, in the love of Jesus. In this way, our mutual relationships become more relaxed and less complicated. In this living with one another and for one another, we sense the blissfully warm breath of God's love. In a word: redeemed as we are, let us also live redeemed.

44

The Virtue of Aging With Dignity

L ast, I turn to the virtue that for me right now, at age eighty-four, is supremely relevant, that is, appreciating and loving the autumn of life, the virtue and art of aging with dignity. I hope to patiently learn it until it leads to the art of all arts, the art of death, or *ars moriendi*, as it was called in the Middle Ages. This virtue is the habit of keeping one's eyes focused on the hour of death and making one's final preparations by exercising all the virtues that are especially suited for the autumn of life. It is the art, so to speak, of daily practicing for death.

First of all, in this context I want to mention something that I have often brought up before, namely the cultivation of a grateful memory. My memory, which once bordered on the fantastic, is slowly but quite perceptibly going. That should not be a reason for complaint, and it never will be if I can keep alive memory's most beautiful treasure, gratitude. We old people have time for frequently recalling our past lives. We can tell one another about the most precious things in our experience and, of course, the bright side and the funny moments.

This memory of the bright side of life brings me to my next point: a sense of humor is quite becoming in old men and women. We can get together and have a good laugh or at least smile at ourselves. I often think that God has shown not just a great deal of patience with me, but humor as well. In many ways he has whispered to me—or actually shouted in my ears—"Bernard, don't take yourself too seriously." When friends tell me or write me, "We still need you," or even, "God still needs you," I can't help laughing heartily and saying, "God spare me the folly of taking myself too seriously." Once we have cheerfully bid farewell to the notion of being irreplaceable, we can feel astonished and grateful to God that he can still make use of us old people. I'll never forget the time that I met a ninety-five-year-old woman who was all bent over. With a dazzling smile she told me: "I believe God can still use us old folks to pray." Her words struck me as a fine sermon: use all that free time of yours to pray!

Advancing old age positively challenges us to keep practicing the virtue of serenity. There are so many things we have to give up. My long walks through the woods and valleys are now a thing of the past. Too bad! Nevertheless every day I walk at least one kilometer outdoors. If I cannot do it at one go, I break it up into several stages.

About five years ago it seemed to me that my vision was rapidly deteriorating. The meticulous eye doctor I went to diagnosed a progressive clouding of the vitreous humor. The fog in front of my eyes grew thicker every day. My ophthalmologist called in a well-known specialist, but he, too, thought there wasn't much to be done. Following Chinese tradition, I began frequently massaging the area around the eyes. The doctor prescribed a remedy made from the bark of ginko trees to improve circulation. Now I can read without glasses once again.

After being hit by violent brain spasms, I was told by both my neurologist and my general practitioner: "Now you absolutely have to stay mentally active; otherwise things will go downhill very quickly." And I followed their advice. I read and keep up with what is going on in the field of theology, especially moral theology. And up till now every year I have written a little book, like this one, and a certain number of articles.

The loss of my voice, which once was strong and resonant, due to the surgical removal of my larynx and part of my trachea, was one more invitation to serenity. But even here the question arose as to what really could or could not be changed. Over the last sixteen years I've given countless lectures with my esophageal substitute-voice, and I've been available as an adviser to many people. At the same time, I've made some progress in keeping silent.

I find it especially painful that I'm losing my hearing. Once again I take this to be an invitation to tranquillity. Still, even here one mustn't simply knuckle under. In old age, the eye of discernment sometimes gets sharper, as if in response to the familiar prayer: "Lord, help me to change what can be changed and to bear what can't. And grant me the art to distinguish between the two."

Like almost all people my age, I find my increasing deafness difficult. Sometimes I have to prick up my ears or ask my conversation partner to speak more clearly. Recently, I told Brother Augustine that I planned to go to the audiologist and possibly ask him for a hearing aid. But he told me how he had managed to do without a hearing aid by rubbing his ears for weeks with a mixture of special herbal oil. I tried it and I have already noted some improvement. At any rate, for the time being, I can wait patiently to see whether a hearing aid might not be useful after all. In such things we old people always have to take into account what is best for our neighbor. If I can fully or at least partly recover my hearing, then I owe that to those around me.

With increasing age, all sorts of ailments and pains set in, but we shouldn't pay too much attention to them. In any event, if we want to grow old with dignity, we must not complain too loud and too often. I think that one helpful principle here—helpful too for the people around us—is to realize that most of the time complaining is exhausting, useless, and a burden on others. By contrast, a positive part of aging with dignity is learning how to listen attentively to other old people, and not showing annoyance if they complain a bit too much. There is a way to listen to a person in pain that is extremely appropriate even for an old man or woman who is hard of hearing.

Dealing reasonably with everything old age brings along is part and parcel of the virtue and art of knowing how to die—which is, after all, the crowning point of our life.

It is one thing to say we all have to die, and another to talk about the grace and virtue of seeing death in the best light. Death should be a beautiful farewell, a final response both to our mortality and to our vocation to eternal life.

I see in successful, dignified aging a constant exercise of the *ars moriendi*. The slow, gradual letting go of the many things we hold dear—without needlessly wasting anything—is a fine thank-you for the gift of life and an anticipation of our last *yes* to the will of God: "Yes, Father, I'm coming, gladly."